Love Made Visible

Love Made Visible

The life and work of Dora Scarlett

Caroline Walker

Dedication

I dedicate this book to my daughters Maya Sophie and Reanna Shanti, who were loved by Dora, and to their father, Keith Walker, who shared with me and our daughters the adventure of our Indian village life.

Contents

FOREWORD

Dora Scarlett was an extraordinary activist and profoundly compassionate human being. When the world was rapidly moving towards urbanisation and industrialisation Dora went to live in rural India to embrace a simple, slow and sustainable way of life. While governments and even aid agencies were advocating economic growth at all costs, Dora pursued the path of rural reconstruction, human wellbeing and social justice. Instead of looking at the rural lifestyle as undeveloped and backward Dora celebrated village culture and the genius of the countryside. She believed that for human happiness quality of life is more important than so-called material living standards.

Dora practised what she believed, living a most modest lifestyle. She totally integrated with the local rural community and devoted her life to the unconditional service of the underprivileged. She was free of personal ambition and ego, a living example of humility, generosity and kindness. She was a great communicator. Her writing style was engaging, accessible, witty and full of insights. I read her newsletters with great pleasure. In those days I was the editor of *Resurgence* magazine, and I was able (at the suggestion of Caroline Walker) to publish these letters from rural India. Our readers hugely appreciated them.

Caroline Walker knew Dora well, and was working in India in a similar spirit. They share much inspiration and imagination, and many ideals and aspirations. I cannot think of anyone better placed to write Dora's biography.

It has been my pleasure and privilege to have known Caroline for more than 30 years. She was caretaker, cook, teacher and the head teacher of the Small School in Hartland where she provided an education involving head, heart and hands to thepupils of rural North Devon. Her whole life has been dedicated to the enhancement of rural life, sustainability and spirituality.

May the life story of Dora Scarlett as told by Caroline Walker entertain, enlighten and inspire those who read this book of timeless values.

Satish Kumar

Chapter 1

AN END AND A BEGINNING

In March, 2001, in South India, an old Englishwoman, recently deceased, is lying in state on a bed of ice and sawdust. Despite the remoteness of the small farm and clinic where she has lived and worked for nearly forty years, thousands of people are gathering there for her funeral. Priests and nuns from local churches and convents have given her the last rites, and have now come to conduct the ceremony. A wooden coffin has been procured, and a six-foot deep pit has been dug and lined with brick so it will support a memorial stone. The body is covered with marigolds and rose garlands, incense is burning and candles have been lit. There is the traditional weeping and wailing of women over the body, while a bottle of gin is being discreetly passed around some of the men who knew and worked with her. A kind of bazaar has appeared in the clinic grounds during the three days of the lying-in-state: people are selling candy-floss, tea stalls have opened up, flowers and fruit are set out. When the time comes for the body to be taken to the grave, people fight for the right to be bearers, and it is taken a long way round, out of the grounds and round by the road, so the teams of pall bearers can carry it, with much pushing and shoving and shouting, in a kind of relay.

So ended the life of Dora Scarlett, MBE, who lived from 1905 to 2001 and whose life embodies several enduring themes from the 20th century. As a young woman Dora was attracted towards Distributism, through the writings of G K Chesterton and Hilaire Belloc. During the Second World War she became a member of the Communist Party. Sent by the Party to be a radio journalist in Hungary, she witnessed first-hand the uprising in 1956 and had to make a hasty escape in a lorry convoy. She wrote and published *Window onto Hungary* in 1957 and resigned from the Communist Party. It was in India where she finally found the authentic life she had been seeking. The writings of Tolstoy, Gandhi and Schumacher inspired her to create Seva Nilayam, Home of Service, where a small farm, that supported a clinic providing free health care for the rural poor, became her home for the rest of her life. She wrote with empathy and deep understanding about the traditional life of the South Indian village at a time of increasing change and modernisation but never romanticised or sensationalised the harshness and poverty around her.

I first met Dora in 1979 when, at the invitation of a friend, John Dalton, who was volunteering as Dora's clinic assistant, my husband and I arrived at Seva Nilayam with a vague idea of finding some work which would enable us to stay in India. We had been, as so many are, both horrified and enchanted by India on two previous six-month visits, and we had found the tourist trail ultimately unsatisfying. Dora's Letters from Seva Nilayam, sent to us by John, painted a picture of good work and simple living to which we were irresistibly drawn. When we met her, Dora was in her mid-seventies, and managing a large staff of Indian and expatriate workers, and seeing hundreds of people every day at the clinic.

I was a little daunted on meeting this legendary figure: she was quite small, heavy-set, wearing Indian clothes, with grey hair tied back in a bun. She was treated with great deference by the staff who called her *periyamma* – "respected older aunt". (In Tamil it is the charming custom to address everyone as if they are members of your extended family: for example, any small boy is *thambi* – "little brother".) She was welcoming to us but made it clear we could stay only for a short time while we looked for other work. Completely unprepared and with no previous experience, I was allowed to help under supervision in the clinic dressing room, treating anything from scabies to leprosy ulcers; my lack of squeamishness proved a great blessing. My husband, equally un-squeamish, learned to do tests with basic equipment in the clinic laboratory.

Health care in the villages of Tamil Nadu, when Dora first arrived, consisted mainly of a man on a bicycle with a couple of syringes and needles and a few ampoules of a cheap antibiotic. These men, often calling themselves "homeopathic doctors" (the certificate could be bought quite cheaply) would cycle around the villages offering injections for a few rupees. Such was the faith in injections (coupled with the fact that many diseases are self-limiting) that these "doctors" had some credibility and plied their trade unchallenged. Provided they had some medical paraphernalia about them and could apply it confidently – even giving intravenous drips in the home, and injecting women through their sari and petticoat to avoid asking them to undress – they could make a living, like the snake-oil salesmen of the Wild West. My six-year-old daughter came in laughing one day from the village to announce she had just seen the *vaityan* (unqualified doctor) applying his stethoscope to the buttocks of a woman complaining of joint pain. These "doctors" often did more harm than good, however, as the antibiotic injection was a sub-clinical dose, potentially promoting antibiotic resistance; and the needles were never properly sterilised, often causing painful complications.

The countryside was littered with small concrete buildings proudly announcing themselves as Government Primary Health Centres; but these buildings were locked, empty, and no staff turned up for work. In the villages there were people suffering from leprosy, TB, and hookworm infestation, who

3

needed proper treatment and careful follow-up. There were babies whose mothers had to work all day and had little milk to give them; or worse, babies who were given a weak solution of milk powder in a dirty bottle and were dying from malnutrition and dehydration caused by gastro-intestinal diseases. Many folk remedies were still current: for jaundice, and anaemia, a coin was heated in the fire and placed on the wrist of the sufferer, causing a painful burn; for measles and chickenpox no treatment was allowed as it was thought to be a disease from the goddess; and for babies who failed to thrive, a dried tree-frog was sewn into a leather pouch and placed around the baby's neck or waist.

Into this far-from-ideal situation came Dora and her volunteers, at first simply walking around the villages with a bag of basic medicines. They visited people in their homes, seeking to understand the patients' situations, and learning about the difficulties of their daily life. Dora's political astuteness made it inevitable that she saw the social and environmental context of ill-health, although she ensured her letters were scrupulously free from political comment. ("I have not dealt at all with the political aspects, as I feel this is the business of Indians themselves, but I have touched on some of the social matters which I believe are holding India back from taking a full share in the life of the world today.") A well-thumbed copy of *Pills against Poverty*, a book by Swedish social anthropologists about medical work in a Tamil village, was passed around the English-speaking clinic staff and served as reminder that without political and social changes, medicine itself was of limited use.

During the 1980s the United Nations was promoting the goal of "Health for All by the Year 2000". This high-flown aspiration was seen by those of us working on the ground in the villages as

4

a far-off goal; *Pills against Poverty* was not the only book pointing out, as Dora often did, that all medical problems are social problems, and the influential work of David Werner in Mexico which produced *Where There is No Doctor* and *Helping Health Workers Learn* sent a strong message that education, followed by community mobilisation for political solutions to poverty and ill-health were the only sustainable way forward. In India, a group of concerned health professionals had established the Medico-Friend Circle (MFC) Bulletin which presented (and still presents today) a refreshingly trenchant critique of provision of health care: "The existing system of health care is not geared towards the needs of the majority of the people, the poor and the rural segments of our society". This was precisely the situation that Seva Nilayam was set up to address, and whilst Dora had no desire to politicise the clinic's work, her views were in agreement with the MFC view that "the health care system is only a part of the total system" and that fundamental changes were needed which would only occur "as part of a total social transformation in the country."

After we had spent a couple of months at Seva Nilayam, Dora introduced us to her friend, Brother James Kimpton, a Christian Brother, in his mid-fifties, who after a successful career as a teacher in the UK, Sri Lanka and India, had felt a call to work with the rural poor, and set up a village development project, Reaching the Unreached of Village India, about two hour's journey from Seva Nilayam. He was a visionary, firmly grounded in the Christian tradition of service, with an impressive range of skills which included architecture, pedagogy, photography, technical training, fine art and water divining. He welcomed volunteers, and invited us to join him. My husband worked in the clinic laboratory and I, after at first working with leprosy patients in the craft workshops, went on

5

to set up and manage the children's nursery and a village health worker training programme. The skills we needed had to be gained from books, manuals and other health workers; Brother James was a constant source of encouragement and raised funds for the ever-expanding work through his newsletters to many international supporters, including "Old Boys" from his Bournemouth teaching days in the 1950s. The often heart- rending stories he told generated large donations from individuals and foundations.

Every day Brother would make his rounds on his Royal Enfield "Bullet" motorcycle, navigating pot-holed roads out into remote villages where people were living in poor mud and thatch huts with no water supply. Wherever he could get agreement from the community, he would build small sturdy concrete houses with neat tiled roofs, use his water-divining skills to indicate the best place for a bore hole and pump, and ensure the new occupants had the titles to their land and house. In larger villages he would repair, or build, a school. Abandoned children were welcomed into purpose-built "Children's Villages", living in small family homes with a foster mother. In addition to the clinic, school, and sheltered workshops on the main campus he also set up a small weaving industry, where unmarried girls could work and save money for their marriage. Older people, especially those disabled by leprosy, with no family to care for them, received a small handout each week and meals from the large community kitchen providing food for the schools and foster families. Brother James had an unshakeable conviction that if the work was good the money would come. Every day he would go to Mass in the local town; every evening he would spend time in prayer in the chapel near his very modest hut. I believe he was an outstanding example of Christian faith in action.

In due course I was elected to the management committee of Seva Nilayam and attended regular meetings there, always accompanied by a good lunch of home-grown produce and a tour of the farm and garden. Dora often voiced her opinion that Brother James' project had become too big, and she kept faithfully to her ideal of "small is beautiful". I could see there were virtues in both approaches. We stayed seven years with Brother James; both my daughters were born during this time. Eventually we felt the need of a new challenge, and our final year in India was spent working, at Dora's suggestion, in the Varusanadu valley where medical care was sparse, and the nearest hospital a long journey by bullock cart.

This remote and beautiful valley had been the home of indigenous tribes until people of the Thevar caste began to move into the area, looking for land suitable for farming. It was said that many of them, including the man who became our landlord, were on the run from the police. They had a reputation for lawlessness, and there was a local saying: "If you are going to Varusanadu, tell your family where your money is hidden, because you may not return." They cleared the forest, using the tribal people as labourers, and planted cotton, groundnuts, and pulses, and grazed their animals. A friend introduced us to one of the elders of Valiparai, Chellandi Thevar.

Valiparai was where the forest began. A wide river flowed down the valley from Meghamalai (Cloud Mountain) on the Kerala border. The nearest bus stop was two hours walk away: only bullock carts or the sturdiest jeeps could negotiate the washed-out roads. On the day we went to ask for permission to live in the village, we walked through a torrential downpour; Chellandi Thevar said this auspicious day of rain convinced him to accept us. We were given two rooms, a kitchen and a

7

verandah in his house, sharing his compound with dogs, chickens and a cow and calf, and his large family who came in and out all day. Every part of the house was made of local mud, stone and wood and the roof was of coconut thatch. The floors were splashed with diluted cow dung every day which left a smooth surface, easy to sweep clean.

We walked around the hills, on paths worn smooth by bare feet, with a local guide and a small supply of basic medicines. Our task was to find people with a persistent cough and test them for TB: if they showed a positive result, we supplied the necessary treatment. We also found children suffering from intestinal disease – most of the drinking water came from the river and there was no sanitation of any kind – and we showed how to make a simple sugar and salt solution for rehydration. We dug our own latrine pit in the field behind the house, to the amusement of the villagers, and we fetched our drinking water from the village pump. We bathed and washed our clothes in the river – until the dry season when the river disappeared. Our two daughters, then aged five and two, had the freedom of the village, playing with the local children, fishing in the river, and collecting wild greens in the fields. When the Forestry Department elephants came past the house, the mahout would lean down and lift the five-year-old up for a ride.

In Valiparai we were privileged to share, as closely as possible, in the life of the village. We discovered that quality of life is not the same as standard of living, and we admired the toughness and resilience of our neighbours, whilst remaining uneasy about the poaching, drug cultivation, illicit alcohol trade, domestic violence and female infanticide that was only too common. After nearly a year in the village, we came to the conclusion that the only solutions to poverty and disease must be political solutions; as foreigners, whose residence permits could be revoked at any time, we could play no part in Indian politics. Fortunately we were offered the opportunity to return to the UK and work in a pioneering educational initiative in a Devon village. This gave us the possibility of continuing our work for change.

Both Brother James and Dora had profound impacts on me as I struggled to address the daily realities of poverty and disease: Brother's open-handed compassion and generosity, aided by his prodigious fund-raising skills, contrasting with Dora's frugal, human-scale, but no less compassionate approach. Both gave me touchstones to guide my own efforts.

Dora was an elegant and accomplished writer, and her *Letters from Seva Nilayam*, newsletters which were sent out periodically to friends and supporters from 1974 to 1994, have been an invaluable resource. Dora was writing her *Letters from Seva Nilayam* at a time when India was emerging into the modern world. And she was writing about an India that was vanishing before her eyes. It is as if she wants to capture what she sees to preserve its value and its beauty because she knows

it will soon be lost. She often laments, in her letters to her brother Frank, the poor quality of the photographs she takes, and how it is impossible to capture the brilliance of the colours, the light and shade, and the detail of people's faces. Before starting the Letters in 1974, this inveterate journalist sends articles to *The Guardian*, the *Liverpool Daily Post*, and short stories to the BBC and to *Blackwood's Magazine*, all sensitive depictions of the life around her. She confides to her friend Alison Selford: "I very much want to write these stories because there is so little writing about Indians (as distinct from stories about Europeans in an Indian setting). Most Europeans here don't live close enough to the Indians to write about them." Her article for the Liverpool newspaper announces proudly: "I am the only European living in the village of Keeraipothampatty." Aware of this uniquely privileged perspective, she is concerned that readers understand the context and history of Indian village life, just as she was at pains, in *Window onto Hungary*, to research Hungarian life and politics so as to give context and meaning to the Uprising.

Her short stories tell of a marriage nearly wrecked by a suspected love potion, of country weddings, of relations between parents, children and servants, of an achingly brief encounter between the son and a former pupil of a missionary, of the tragedy of leprosy in a family: village lives and landscapes closely observed and set out without sensationalism or mawkish sentimentality. *Blackwood's Magazine* published three stories (*The Last House in the Town*, *The Waterfall*, and *Guidance*) in 1963 as *South Indian Sketches*; and *The Servant* was broadcast by the World Service in 1985. A proposed book on Mudichur, mentioned in 1962, did not materialise, but lengthy descriptions of Mudichur were included in the later chapters of her unpublished *Memoir*. Once her *Letters from Seva Nilayam* started their regular circulation this seems to have given Dora the outlet she craved and an audience who were sympathetic to her work. Satish Kumar published some of the Letters in editions of *Resurgence* magazine during the 1980s under the title *Letter from South India*. Otherwise the Letters were sent to a lengthy mailing list of supporters all over the world and bound into booklets for sale, the profits going to *Village Service Trust*, the charity set up in the UK to support Seva Nilayam and its partners.

The many forms of religious life in India intrigued and inspired her, and she was particularly fond of (though never wrote in the *Letters* about) Dom Bede Griffiths, an English Benedictine monk, whose ashram on the banks of the river Cauvery she visited numerous times, particularly enjoying the very extensive library, private conversations with Father Bede about spiritual matters, and the opportunity to advise him on his garden. My first visit there, one of many, was with a box of plants sent by Dora to restock his garden after the 1979 cyclone had washed it away. In this ashram Christian practice was integrated with the ways of Indian temple worship – an authentic dialogue between east and west of which Dora thoroughly approved. She particularly liked the Sanskrit chants and asked to have recordings of them. The monks wore Indian dress, lived in simple huts, kept cows, and practised yoga. Both my daughters were baptised by Father Bede in ceremonies which he devised especially for them with readings from the *Upanishads* and Indian music.

In many respects Dora was recording a vanishing world, and of course it has to be acknowledged that not all that was vanishing was worth keeping: great strides have been made in the status of women, even in areas local to Seva Nilayam known for female infanticide, early marriage and gender discrimination. Many years of patient work by projects inspired by Seva Nilayam have resulted in a network of women's self-help groups and women's federations, working to improve the financial and social status of women. These groups challenge discrimination, encourage lower-caste women (even in the face of death threats) to stand for public office, promote the avoidance of early marriage and provide low cost loans for women to start businesses. Education is now the norm for girls as well as boys, with far fewer working children and far fewer child marriages.

Visitors to India today will see that the beautiful brass and clay pots celebrated by Dora, products of hundreds of years of craftsmanship, are now mostly replaced for daily use by garishly coloured plastic vessels – lighter to carry, it must be admitted, but not pleasing to the eye. Brass pots are still given as gifts, but rarely leave the house to go to the well – many houses have piped water now. The fragility of clay pots, which guaranteed continued work for the potters, is no longer appreciated. The virtually indestructible old granite grindstones now lie upturned and abandoned in front of many houses, having been replaced by electric grinders and mixers. Indeed, in the late 1980's Dora wrote to me, half-triumphantly and half- apologetically, to tell me they had been given an electric idli-grinder, making light work of the preparation of the steamed lentil and rice cakes which used to take many hours. The brooms and baskets made from coconut ribs and fragrant grasses by traditional artisans, by custom thrown away, to break down harmlessly or be put on the fire, and replaced each Pongal festival with new ones, now have plastic equivalents, which, when no longer usable, are thrown on village rubbish heaps where they sit with other waste until they are burnt, releasing toxic fumes into the air.

Travel is no longer by bullock cart; auto rickshaws carrying unfeasible numbers of people and alarmingly large loads of goods have replaced them. Villages only a bullock cart could reach in the old days, navigating washed-out culverts and deep ruts, are now served by buses and autos. Buses can still get astonishingly crowded, the conductor pushing his way through tightly packed passengers to collect the fares: but private cars and motorbikes, once very rare sights which caused a stir if they arrived in the village, are everywhere. Large numbers of brightly painted lorries and tourist minibuses speed along the much-improved road system, while the legendary Indian railway trains, where seats and berths can now be booked on-line, still offer the unique experience enjoyed by Dora on her travels.

In the 1980s Dora could state confidently that there is "no serious litter problem" in South Indian villages, but this is unfortunately no longer true; following the proliferation of factory-made and packaged consumer goods, village lanes, ditches and hedges are now lined with multi-coloured remnants of plastic bags, bottles, sachets, wrappings and rags, amongst which crows, chickens, pigs, dogs, goats and cows scratch for edible morsels.

The tribal people depicted by Dora as "primeval innocents" are now seldom seen hunting wild animals and gathering honey, fruits, and medicinal plants. In one of her early letters to Alison, responding to concerns about a possible Chinese invasion of India, Dora, unperturbed, writes "if the Chinese come, I will go and live with a hill tribe near here. They are friendly little people ... and no one has bothered about them since the dawn of existence." In the twenty-first century, however, pushed to the margins by the clearing of the hills for agriculture, and harassed by forest guards if they try to practise their traditional occupations, tribal people suffer serious deprivation and are vulnerable to alcoholism and mental illness. Tribal children living far from the road find it difficult to get to school and face at times the threat of wild animals and swollen rivers. The discrimination they experience leads to a high drop-out rate: this is one of the challenges that *Village Service Trust* is addressing in its current work.

I have always felt Dora's story deserved to be known. This biography is based on a *Memoir* written by her in the 1970's which was never published and came to me, after she died, in rather tattered bundles of typed foolscap. The memoir ends in 1962 when she leaves Mudichur village to begin a new life at

Seva Nilayam.

I have almost a full set of letters from the 1950s to the 1990s between Dora and Alison Selford, an old friend and fellow ex-Communist. Alison meticulously kept carbon copies of both typewritten and handwritten letters to Dora and generously donated them to *Village Service Trust*. I met her in her residential home in Highgate in July 2017 – a home famous for the fact that many of its inmates are old left-wingers of various kinds. Although aged 97, with poor eyesight, she gave me a long and fascinating interview. Reading these frank and often humorous letters gives a valuable insight into Dora's situation and state of mind. They are especially interesting as they record Dora's first impressions of Sri Lanka and India. I also have letters to her brother, Frank Scarlett, and her Hungarian friend, Laci Gondor. I have my own memories of Dora: I worked in India from 1979 to 1987 and regularly went to Seva Nilayam as a committee member and a friend. She encouraged my writing and was always ready with advice on the issues I encountered in the course of my work. I last saw her on a family visit to India in 1995, as I describe later. I have conducted interviews with people closely associated with Dora to complete the final chapter.

The first six chapters of this book tell the story of Dora's life drawn from these various sources; the subsequent chapters are arranged thematically and quote extensively from Dora's *Letters from Seva Nilayam*, which stopped in 1995. The final chapter tells the story of Dora's final years.

We begin with Dora's introduction to her unpublished *Memoir*.

When I look back on my life, and think how events have shaped themselves over the years, and how my thoughts and feelings have developed, I seem to find two main principles which recur throughout. One is that nothing is wasted, and the other is that there are no short cuts.

Life is like a thrifty housewife, who stuffs into her rag-bag or stows in her lumber room all kinds of strange oddments of experience, along with endeavours that ended in failure, and mistakes and follies. All these seemed to me quite useless, and I would gladly have buried them for ever, but a day came when life brought them out, and said: "The very thing you want. You threw it away, but I kept it."

And as regards short cuts – I am sure that many people who find a book that alters their lives, or meet a person who comes to mean a great deal to them, say: "How I wish I had read this years ago! How I wish I had met you earlier!" But years earlier the book would have been no use, it would not have yielded up its treasures, and the person would probably not have been attracted by our friendship. So we have to wait, accepting the fact that any true growth must be slow; we have to take things as they come, and let them fall into pattern like a kaleidoscope that is turned.

A few years ago a good friend urged me strongly to write my autobiography. I resisted the idea, saying that I was not a sufficiently noteworthy person, but half-consciously because I knew I was not ready. I am sure, if I had written it then, I would later have been dissatisfied with it. Aldous Huxley once said that he never liked reading anything he had written years before. If he agreed with it, he thought: "I haven't developed at all", and if he disagreed with it, he thought: "What a fool I was then." I feel rather like this regarding both things I wrote in the past and the larger number of things I refrained from writing. So how do I know that I can write now?

Because I have felt a growing conviction that I have passed a certain point from which the landscape, when I look back on it, has a shape and a meaning. I can at last see where the rivers run, and where the roads lead, as I could not do when I was still struggling through bogs and thickets. It would be false humility for me to say that I doubt whether what I write can be of use or interest to anyone. Life, from the time of my earliest recollections, has been of absorbing interest to me, and I feel that if I describe it faithfully it will be interesting enough for others to wish to read.

Chapter 2

<hr>

BORN A NORTHENER

I was born a northerner, and grew up with a Liverpool accent, a strong provincial pride in my city, a feeling for the sea, and a sympathy with the Irish.

Dora May Scarlett was born on the 29th of December 1905, in a house in the suburbs of Liverpool. The family had moved there from London where Robert Scarlett, her father, had taught in academies for young gentlemen. Her grandparents were working class: Dora's maternal grandmother, from High Wycombe, left an orphan at seventeen by a great cholera epidemic which killed both her farm-labourer parents, became a servant in a gentleman's house. There she met her husband, also a servant, and like many other rural people they joined the great migration to London, settling in Factory Square, Streatham. Dora's maternal grandfather was an ostler at the Pied Bull Inn, and Dora's grandmother supplemented his small wage with taking in washing, and sitting up with sick people at night. Dora's mother and her three sisters left school at the age of twelve and went into domestic service.

On her father's side, a touching anecdote had been passed down through the family:

"My paternal great-grandfather was a stonemason in Enniskillen. His son, my grandfather was something of a rolling stone ... He became a sergeant in the Guards at Buckingham Palace, and wore a tall black busby and a scarlet tunic.

"One day, Queen Victoria, driving by the barracks, heard the sound, unmistakable to a maternal ear, of whooping

17

cough. She stopped her carriage to ask who was coughing, and was told it was Sergeant Scarlett's little boy. Next morning she sent a footman to enquire after the child. The boy was Robert Scarlett, my father, and one of four brothers. This story was never forgotten in the family."

From this and other stories – "my aunt once saw the great Queen, and reported that she was very small, and 'looked like a short, fat cook' but the remark was made with affection" – Dora, experiencing "the last ripples of that immense wave of emotion and loyalty that surrounded Queen Victoria in her later years" was, as a child, conscious of "power and majesty, mingled with warm domesticity, an acceptance of life as it was, and complete ignorance of the world outside".

The sickly baby, Robert Scarlett, Dora's father, became a studious and quiet boy. As an external student he took a degree, a thing unheard of in his family, and achieved a BSc from London University. After his marriage he taught in private schools in Holland Park and Horsham, finally moving to Liverpool to take up a post as a mathematics and physics teacher in a secondary school. Dora loved the story of how, "my mother's mother, when she heard of the new appointment, said: 'But, my dear, you will surely never go so far away from home?' My mother staunchly replied: 'But it will be my home'."

"My parents first got lodgings in Parliament Street, which is one of the older parts of the city, where elegant houses of the old cotton merchants were sinking into decrepitude. My mother had never heard ships' sirens, and the first time she heard a hooting from the river she froze in horror, unable to imagine what the sound could be. It was like the dying bellow of a gigantic cow. But it was not long before the various notes and pitches of ships' sirens became a commonplace of life."

They moved to Wavertree, first to Borrowdale Road and then to Kenmare Road, a district of red brick terraces with whitened steps. The dining room was her father's study, lined with books, and outside a back yard, where Dora attempted to grow a few flowers, and a cobbled back alley.

"From this unremarkable suburb a half-hour ride in the tram – the clanging, grinding electric trams, that screeched round bends – led to the Pier Head and the broad Mersey estuary, an arm of the sea five miles wide, and filled with the shipping of almost every country in the world. There was excitement in stepping on the mile-long floating landing stage, which rose and fell with the tides, and vibrated with the landing of ships. We could watch the P&O and White Star liners come in, but even more interesting were the smaller vessels, bearing strange names, and flags which we had to look up in the back of the atlas, and brown-faced sailors who threw buckets of kitchen waste overboard, while a crowd of gulls descended, screaming and flapping, to snap up everything eatable. On holidays we could go 'across the water' in one of the broad, tub-like ferry boats, which took horses and carts, and lorries, as well as passengers; on the other side we reached New Brighton which was really an extension of Liverpool suburbs, but had a sandy beach on which we could have donkey rides, out past the battery which guarded the Mersey Bar, and marked the point where the Irish Sea began. Seen from across the water, Liverpool lay always under a haze of coal smoke.

"Between the Mersey and the rows and rows of dim brick-built, slate-roofed houses that made up the poorer quarters of Liverpool lay a region of great warehouses lining the Dock Road. This part of the city was quiet, as there were no houses there, and the buildings were cliff-like, with sunlight slanting between them, to where the pigeons, white and brown and blue- green, picked among the chaff fallen from the horses' nose- bags. Many of the streets were paved with cobble-stones, and the loaded drays came rumbling along, drawn by the mighty horses, whose shoes clashed on the stones. Such horses were the pride and joy of the draymen, and even on ordinary working days they had their tails and manes plaited, and their brass ornaments (which, I have heard, date from the traditions of the Crusaders) gleaming and sparkling.

"But on the First of May there was a great parade of horses on St. George's Plateau, with the Lord Mayor presenting prizes for the best, and best groomed, and best decorated horses. Then their manes were plaited with flowers, and they had plumes on their heads and all kinds of gay trappings on their backs. My father always took me to see the May Horses, and one of my earliest memories is of him lifting me above the crowd to see these glorious monsters. Among us children, if anyone seemed overdressed, the saying was: 'You're all dressed up like a May Horse'. But down in their working area of dockland, it was exciting to see that many loads were of cotton, which would be going to the spinning towns of South Lancashire; or to see sacks of wheat hoisted on ropes to a dizzy height, and disappear into the hatch at the top storey of the warehouse. This was all a child's-eye view, but I think that from a very early age I was deeply interested in seeing what was going on in the world ..."

A love of plants was nurtured by visits to Sefton Park Palm House, a paradise "with delicate creepers trailing up the pillars; plants in pots were banked to form a sea of colour. I can feel now the way the brass door handles turned, and smell the warm but temperate atmosphere, full of sweet scents; what gardeners call a 'buoyant' atmosphere, especially pleasing when the weather was harsh outside."

Her father encouraged her growing love of books:

"In *Flowers of Many Lands* there was a plate with a bouquet of Indian flowers, containing the beautiful rich blue 'shell' flower, which climbs in the hedges of my Indian garden today, and in *Economic Botany* I saw how nutmegs, cloves, coffee, and ginger grow – all a familiar sight to me here in South India. My father also introduced me to *Just-So Stories*, which he illustrated for me himself on a series of cards; to the *Jungle Books* and, not least, to *Kim*, which I did not understand, but later read avidly."

In 1916 Dora's brother, David, nine years older than her, a corporal in the King's Liverpool Regiment, was killed at the Battle of the Somme.

"The war was like an overshadowing presence, whose wings stretched from horizon to horizon; daily life went on, with fun and affection and hope, but everything smelt of war, tasted of war, and was coloured by war.

"In the Smithdown Road, where we did our shopping, was a pork butcher's shop. It was owned by a German couple named Rutch. It was a clean and orderly shop, and the Rutches were clean and orderly people. The meats they sold were prepared on the premises – boiled ham, jellied veal, sausages, black puddings and white puddings. At one end of the counter was a large earthenware pan, unglazed on the outside and yellow glazed inside, of a kind much used in Lancashire then. It was full of savoury pork dripping.

"One day, passing near this shop, I saw a crowd. The plate glass window was shattered, and all the utensils thrown into the street. The Rutches lived in the room above the shop, and a piano had been thrown down from the upper window and broken. A soldier was sitting at it and playing something on the jangled keys, while the crowd roared with laughter. I fled down one of the back entries, and there I saw the great pan of dripping smashed in the dirt. I have seen much more violence and hatred in my life since then, but scarcely anything more foolish and pathetic."

Shortly after the end of the war Dora's father died, aged 53, leaving her mother to bring up Dora, and a cousin, Frank, two years older, who had been adopted into the family. She took in lodgers, and was helped by her husband's friends. A maintenance grant enabled Dora to stay on at secondary school. It was assumed that she would become a teacher, the obvious choice for a girl who was too well-educated to join the "hordes of typists, hairdressers and shop assistants". But Dora was convinced that "academic life was a trap; I was in danger of walking into a prison. I felt that real life lay outside the academic circle. ... I was a 'drop-out' before the term was invented."

"If I had been able to put some part of my thought into words, it might have been like this: 'Book learning tells you a lot about the world, but it isn't the world. I have had some book learning and I am glad of it. I have also learnt something more important, which is how to teach myself anything further I want to know. But I want to get into the world, even if I have to wash dishes and scrub floors'."

Following her father's example, she read widely, "with a talent for getting the guts out of a book, for savouring the undertones and overtones of historical period, the interplay of belief, custom and habit, and relishing the sights, the sounds, the very air and earth of countries however remote".

"I read without plan. I read the *Dialogues* of Plato, and tried to read Kant. I followed the travels of Marco Polo on the map, and only lost the trail among the cities of China, some of which had names I could not find on the maps of today. I loved Chaucer; I thought I ought to admire Blake, but found him forbidding, yet somehow intimate; I read Rabelais, the *Decameron*, Keats and Shelley; Thomas Hardy, Thackeray ... and Gerard Manley Hopkins; *All Quiet on the Western Front*, *The Constant Nymph*, and *The Story of an African Farm*; scores of novels, histories and travel books the names of which I have forgotten. So much mixed and indiscriminate reading was spread over the years from my fourteenth to twentieth, but although much of it was beyond my understanding at the time, what I understood I did assimilate.

"I had periods when I desperately longed to be quite conventional, to be popular at dances and to be included in the office conversation about silk stockings, film stars and cosmetics. But I was shy and awkward, and everybody seemed to regard me as being a bit out of touch with life. I could make friends, but there was always a slight falsity in the relationship, one note out of tune. This was because I made friends in order to have friends, not because of real affection for the person. I have since learnt that any disingenuousness, however slight, cannot be hidden, and no sound relationship can be built if it exists."

A few years before his death her father joined the Catholic Church, and regularly attended early Mass, sometimes taking young Dora with him. Always curious, Dora observed closely the actions and reactions of the priest and people, noting a "complete liberty for anyone to do what he liked in the way of devotion", and a great variety of class and social standing among the worshippers, contrasting it with her experience at Church of England services where everyone stood, sang or sat at the same time.

"Hinduism, as I have found out now, is, like Catholicism, a house of many mansions, where all sorts can be at home. Children play in temples unreproved, and those who have made a long pilgrimage sit down and eat their food, and even do their washing and hang it up to dry. It is common to find someone fast asleep in a corner; many make their circumambulations of the holy of holies; one may bow down in an agony of desire for God – the 'One without a second, beyond thought, beyond knowledge, without name or form' – while another may see divinity in a statue of a being with six arms or an elephant's head. The priest opens the inner shrine, lights the lamps, rings the bell, utters Sanskrit chants, offers flowers and fruits, and comes out to distribute sacred ashes and rose petals to a little knot of assembled worshippers; this done, each returns to his own thoughts.

"I have had in my life many vicissitudes of belief and disbelief, but I have always thought that if man must worship – as it seems he must – this is the right way to do it. Experience of the Catholic Church has taught me to understand the jolly cartloads of Indian peasants who go off, cooking pots and all, to some far- off mountain temple, and the little groups of people – shopkeepers, business men, school children and beggars – who congregate round the shrines in the streets in the early morning."

Dora was about fifteen when she became a Catholic, a member of a "weighty and influential" minority in Liverpool. She remembered going with her mother on a thousand-strong pilgrimage to Lourdes and never forgot their return into a gigantic welcoming crowd on St George's Plateau singing *Faith of our Fathers*.

"Between the ages of fifteen and twenty-five I had many periods of recurrent doubt, but I discovered that Catholics are remarkably resilient in intellectual difficulties about faith, partly because the Church can mean so much to them that they cannot face doing without it; partly because their religion is so many-sided that they can dwell on aspects which they find safer, and meanwhile trust that there will be some explanation; also because they believe in a personal Devil and are afraid that what they are experiencing is a snare laid by him. In my experience I have found that those who leave the Church are more often influenced by sheer worldliness which leads them into a state where religion, if it means anything at all, is only on the periphery of life. Those to whom it seems important to answer the questions posed by life ... will suffer agonies and go through periods of black despair, but still cling to the belief which causes their torments, because it seems the only way in which an answer can be hoped for.

"It was through Catholicism, and through the social and

political outlook founded on it, that I came into contact with the Distributist movement of Hilaire Belloc and G K Chesterton. This was a new revelation, but very much in line with what I seemed always to have craved for."

"Belloc did me the service of forcing me to think about real things; until I read his writing, I had followed the childish habit of thinking about labels," she wrote. Distributism appealed to her because it identified

"... a pattern of society which seemed the ideal. It was a society based on the widespread ownership of small property, which was the best safeguard of liberty. ... In a society where the miller owns his mill, the blacksmith his forge, the farmer his fields, and the baker his ovens, people can live while defying oppression. This would be the keynote of Distributist society, and it had flourished once in reality, in mediaeval Europe. Belloc and Chesterton were not fanciful enough to think that a return could be made to precisely those conditions, that people must use locally made candles instead of electricity, and must employ a local runner to deliver letters. But they said that if small private ownership were widespread enough to be the norm of society it would not only secure greater liberty but bring about a genuine revival of craftsmanship. It would not be the dilettantism of people who make their living working for some vast corporation, and do weaving or woodcarving as escapism; craftsmanship would arise from the conditions of life itself. Everything which could not because of its nature be owned by individuals, such as electricity and telephones, should be nationalised, but production of clothing, food and tools, printing and building, could be done by those who owned the means of production, and almost all of the real needs of man could be satisfied."

What made Belloc's prophecy more credible was the coming of the Great Depression.

"Sometimes in the course of a morning there would be nine or ten knocks at our house door, and each time a worn and seedy-looking man would open a cheap suitcase containing combs, needles, hairpins, or small kitchen gadgets – and he would explain how desperate he was because of months or years of unemployment. Sometimes it would not be even a suitcase but a flimsy cardboard box containing packets of lavender or papers of pins. We had moved out to a 'Garden Suburb' where we had a small garden patch and a few shrubs and trees. If the unemployed man had nothing to sell, he would offer to put in an hour's work trimming the grass and hedges. Others would ask for a brass object to polish or a broken china cup to stick with some liquid or glue, and others would open a tin and start to polish the floor just inside the front door as a demonstration. Once they had actually mended or polished something it was difficult to turn them away. Some brought nothing at all, but just begged. Begging was illegal, but the sale of lavender and packets of pins was only thinly concealed begging. It was impossible to give only the halfpenny which was about all they were worth - the minimum was twopence, and my mother often gave sixpence. We bought far more needles and hairpins than we could ever use, and our drawers and cupboards were reeking with lavender. My mother never wanted to turn anybody away. Someone once said to her, 'A lot of these people aren't genuine, they are making more money than you think', and I have never forgotten her reply: 'I would rather be deceived sometimes than turn away anybody in need'."

This principle Dora would carry with her for the rest of her life. The Depression confirmed her conviction that "Capitalism was mad; it had reached its limit; it was unworkable." She recalls the excitement she felt on finding others whose views were so near her own heart, and the values and principles that she was to put into practice at Seva Nilayam many years later were learned and developed during this hard time, and articulated in this way:

> "I had always felt that the elementary needs of mankind, the open air, the seas and rivers, the green earth and all its fruits, were the source of all beauty and satisfaction and that the farther one went away from nature, the more dangerous, futile and unsatisfying life became. To this, as a Catholic and Distributist, I could add the ethic of ownership as trusteeship, and work as worship."

Much as she admired Belloc and Chesterton, Dora imagined that a new society would only come about "by the collapse of our present one, a new dark age, and a rebirth".

Dora later reflected:

> "Very much has happened since then, an end to the Great Depression, a second World War, an undreamed-of advance in technology, and a whole set of new problems, concerning nuclear weapons, population and pollution. The world is less secure; people are more afraid, more bewildered and more discontented. Belloc and Chesterton have been borne away on the rolling stream of time; yet I think this mental fight was not wasted, and has its relevance today."

Dora and her mother c.1909

Chapter 3

A DEVONSHIRE SMALLHOLDER

*An aptitude for the practical things of life, acquired in
early years, is a precious gift.*

Dora left school at sixteen, "to the disgust of teachers and
friends" and took a succession of office jobs, which she did
not enjoy. Fortunately, in her early twenties, she saw a chance
to fulfil a long-held desire to live in the country. She moved to
Oxfordshire, and as part of a team of four young women, with
only food and basic accommodation provided, learned skills of
farm work and poultry keeping which she would use for the rest
of her life.

Despite the hardship, "the country was glorious, and I exulted in
the open-air life". At the end of the training she moved to
Devon. The joy of this new life is evident:

"I managed to buy a small cottage in Devonshire, very
cheaply, because it was not on any road, but approached
only by a stile path, and with about an acre of ground
through which ran a small stream with banks full of wild
daffodils. The cottage must have been about two hundred
years old, and was built of clay ('cob' as it is called in
Devonshire) with a roof of heavy tiles, doors like yard
doors, with old iron latches, and walls three feet thick
inset with deep window seats. It has interested me to find
in India the same distinction between the clay, or *kutcha*
houses, and the brick or stone built *pukka* houses, as in
south- west England between the cob and the brick
houses. I started my independent life in a kutcha house,

and I live in a kutcha house now, having lived in many pukka houses in between. My mother, who was now an old age pensioner, came to join and help me.

"The life suited me. I was able to use my practical bent to the full. I was not playing at rusticity while living on independent means; I found that I could pay my way while producing a good part of our own food. I learned to prune, bud and graft fruit trees, to pick and store apples; to grow good vegetables; to keep pigs and salt the bacon; to rear chickens and ducks; I could even use a scythe for cutting grass, and found great pleasure in it. Later on, and during the Second World War, when I had taken on a rather larger holding, I kept a few sheep, and also started bee-keeping. I could take and hive a swarm without trepidation, and I found that the apple honey harvest, and the double clover harvest of mid-Devon gave rich rewards. I still think that bee- keeping is one of the most intensely interesting occupations in the world ..."

She observed both the rural life around her and her own development with an unflinching eye. Having decided to do what was in her own nature, rather than copy others, she had the feeling she was on the road to self-discovery. The interested and sympathetic gaze she turned on Devonshire locals she would later turn on South Indian villagers in her Letters from Seva Nilayam.

"The older generation of villagers in that remote corner of England were simpler, more rustic and less educated than any you would find today. Few had radio sets and none had television. Many had not been away from their farms for a single day in twenty or thirty years. They had often gone to market, but always returned in time to do the

31

milking. They believed in the evil eye and in the efficacy of curses, and they held to that idea, as old as humanity itself, that if you praise anything unduly it will meet with misfortune. If a hen brought out an extra fine and numerous brood of chickens they were wary of showing them. If they owned a very special cow, they would not encourage praise: 'Her's a good milker, her is,' was enough to say. Always play safe where the unknown powers are concerned.

"They made the best clotted cream I have ever tasted. I could buy it at the farm for ninepence a pound (that is, of course, the old currency, not the ninepence of today) and I could go into the dim, shaded dairy to see the thick butter-yellow crusts skimmed off the standing pans. These people had many skills in hedging, ditching, thatching, haymaking and dairying. With the countryman's traditional caution, they would never tell you how much money they made, although market prices were among the commonest topics of discussion. They worked hard for everything they made, and they were seldom dishonest."

It is difficult to discern, from her writings and from friends' observations, any reference to a romantic relationship with anyone. Dora gives no more than a hint that perhaps at this time some liaisons may have occurred:

"There are many things in this period of my life which now cause me to feel ashamed, and which I would rather forget. These arose mainly from the fact that I had found my feet for the first time, and had lost my shyness; I was exhilarated and self-confident. I was living among people much less educated than myself, and it was easy to make an impression on them. I think my position, as a young woman making her own way in the world, with the slenderest of means, and apparently plenty of courage, gave me a very strong appeal to anyone with naturally tender or chivalrous feelings. I let myself be led into some relationships which were not creditable to me or kind to others."

She appears to have found a deep satisfaction in the simplicity and self-sufficiency of this life:

"The monetary rewards of all this work were very small, but I was never in debt, and we had an abundance of good food. We often sat down to a table on which everything but the sugar and salt was home produced: it might be roast chicken, with big dishes of vegetables, salads, brown potatoes, baked apples or stewed plums".

At this time her brother Frank was a subscriber to the *Daily Worker*, the organ of the Communist Party of Great Britain. He would send them in bundles to her, and they were a revelation:

"The people who wrote this paper seemed to have views which made more sense than any I had met since I reluctantly gave up my hopes of Distributism. On all the news of the day (or, of weeks ago, since I received the papers only when a large batch had accumulated) they seemed to be able at once to take up a very definite position, and to express views which were startlingly new to me, yet carried the stamp of consistency and common sense. I did not know then that such consistency was often achieved by suppressing awkward or unpalatable facts ... I thought that the actions of those who set out to lead the workers, the poor and the oppressed classes, must of their very nature be clear, honest and unequivocal for what was to be gained by any other course? The *Daily Worker* sounded as honest as this."

Dora had seen in the Great Depression how capitalism "could not give daily bread to the weary men who came selling pins and lavender at our door". She knew that if she had read Marx at an earlier time in her life, she would not have understood him, but now the time is right.

"I read the *Communist Manifesto*, and from its first words: 'A spectre is haunting Europe – the spectre of Communism' to its last: 'The death knell of Capitalism is sounded – the expropriators are expropriated' I felt that this was what I had been waiting to hear. ... I read Marx's *Capital*, and I began to see, even if dimly, the vast energies of the working class movement; the gruelling intellectual labour of those who fashioned its theory; the courage of those who refused all easy solutions and soft compromises; the loyalty of the workers to each other and to their movement, a loyalty which crossed national frontiers; decades of suffering and of hope; the abortive revolutions which failed because they came before their time; the single-mindedness of those to whom the wealth, art and beauty of the capitalist world meant nothing, because the only beauty was in the red star which had already risen over the Soviet Union.

"I was like someone who has been travelling within sight of a great mountain range, which is yet invisible because hidden in mist. Suddenly the clouds part, as if a curtain had been withdrawn, and the glittering peaks are revealed in all their majesty. Such an experience is unforgettable in relation to solid, material mountains, and equally unforgettable in the country of the mind."

Marx provided her with an intellectual framework with which to understand the world and great movements of history, and the individual's place in it.

"Here was a theory of the world and its development which was tough, resilient, and reasoned all through. No sentimentality, no platitudes, no reliance on miracles ... Marxism (or dialectical materialism) taught that change was continual throughout nature, and that part of nature which we call human affairs. It is inescapable. Nothing is fixed, no social system, no philosophy, morality, religion, economic activity or form of government. We act on our environment to change it, and in the process, it changes us."

Then, once again, world history erupted into Dora's life:

"I was sitting on a warm September day in a quiet garden where the apples were ripening, when I heard that we were at war with Germany."

The *Daily Worker* opposed the war, on the grounds it was a phony war, and in January 1941 the paper was banned. Dora's stubborn and non-conformist nature was galvanised: "I was not a pacifist, but I did not think people should be forced to fight a war which they did not choose to wage, and were not allowed to criticise. I have felt, many times in my life, that it is an honour to be on the side of those who merit the displeasure of Authority."

On the back of a Communist pamphlet she saw a small coupon with the words "I want to join the Communist Party" and a space for name and address. She filled it in and sent it to the Party headquarters and waited to see what would happen.

Chapter 4

A PARTY WORKER

This was a time I could toughen up my thinking.

Dora's introduction to the Communist Party was decidedly underwhelming:

> "I received a letter asking me to call at the house of the local Party secretary. The door was opened by the secretary's wife, a young woman wearing slacks, smoking a cigarette, and with a dull and dirty looking scarf wound turban-wise around her head. There was nothing wrong with the costume itself – it was the usual wear for war-time – but she had a general air of slovenliness, and I did not like people who could not be bothered to take a cigarette out of their mouths before opening the door to a visitor."

Despite the undeniable thrill she felt at being called "comrade" for the first time, she was not impressed by the uncleared dinner table, and the crumbs between the pages of the pamphlets she took home. She began to attend local party meetings, which were usually only of five or six people, but she enjoyed "a frank give and take of ideas, and a recognition that all differences were small beside the loyalties and ideals held in common".

So began Dora's complicated relationship with the Communist Party. She had no idea how she could be of use, and writes with a wry amusement about the suggestion that she try to recruit local agricultural labourers into a Union:

> "I was very perturbed at this, although I could not, myself, think of any other work I could do. But could I do this? It seemed very unlikely. I had never been a member of a Trade Union, and knew nothing about organising one. There was no existing Agricultural Workers' Union within reach, so no chance of offering help or learning from one that was already a going concern. I imagined myself going along one of our beautiful Devon lanes, between high banks glowing with primroses, bluebells and purple orchids, and overarched with hazel bushes, and looking out for a hedger or ditcher, or someone opening a gate for a flock of sheep, and seizing on him with the question: 'Have you ever thought about joining the Union?' The answer would undoubtedly be 'I can't say as I has'. And there I would be as stuck as he would be."

Dora recognised that her credentials as a party worker were slim: she had never worked in a trade union or factory. She was there from conviction, rather than experience, and knew that to the majority of the country the party's views on the war were anti-patriotic, even treacherous. The British CP was made up mainly of intellectuals, rather than workers, and had little influence:

> "I remember one Party Secretary writing in a news sheet: 'The working class is swinging into action with the Communist Party at its head', but this was not noticed by anybody else."

"However," writes Dora, "this was a time when I could toughen up my thinking", and she appreciated the chance to drop unrealistic and utopian notions, concentrating only on strengthening the party and working for the hoped-for revolution.

There was a turning point in June 1941 when Hitler attacked the Soviet Union, prompting the CP general secretary, Harry Pollitt, to declare that it was now a People's War, because the leader of the international working class was involved. The ban was lifted from the *Daily Worker* and the party faithful felt vindicated. Dora continued to try to reconcile notions of patriotism on the one hand and commitment to international class struggle on the other:

> "Lenin said: 'The workers have no Fatherland', meaning that to bring about the proletarian revolution their loyalty must be to the international working class, and not to the capitalist class of their own countries, which would send them like sheep to the slaughter for the sake of colonial possessions, raw materials and markets. It had happened. My brother enlisted in 1914 in the glow of patriotism, urged on by flag-wagging and the preaching of hate against the Kaiser; I do not think he ever knew what he died for in the hopeless mud of the Somme in 1916. 'Patriotism is not enough'."

With hindsight, it was possible for Dora to acknowledge the reality of the Stalinist regime to which the Party turned a blind eye:

> "Over large areas the cruelties of Stalin had made masses of people ready to go over to the invaders, and they changed their minds only when they found that the invaders also were killers of the innocent, looters and tyrants. After the war, thousands upon thousands of soldiers who had been encircled by German troops, taken

prisoner or deported to Germany, found, when they at last came home, that instead of being in the arms of their families they were in prisoner convoys headed for forced labour camps – only because Stalin thought that no one who had been in contact with the capitalist world could be trusted."

Dora's local Party members campaigned for the Labour candidate in the 1945 election, and there was a landslide victory: "It really seemed as if life was beginning anew".

Dora began German lessons with a Jewish refugee, originally from the Sudetenland, who had fled to Britain and had found it impossible to return to Czechoslovakia because she only spoke German. "She was one of those unfortunate people who lost every move in the terrible game played over Europe. ... But her life gave me some understanding of the endless human complications and complexities that occur in any political upheaval, and taught me that people cannot be pigeonholed, or judged as black or white." In a handwritten note on an early version of the memoir Dora then commented, "In the end she committed suicide".

She met a young woman from Prague who worked for the Czech CP. Dora asked if she could visit, and it was agreed. She planned to go to the 1948 Sokol Festival, which was to be a joyful celebration of Czech independence and peace.

"Yet when I applied for a visa, I received no reply. I wrote a number of times, then at last I composed a long political and personal letter to the Consul General, stating that I was a member of the British Communist Party, and asking, in effect, what his Government was playing at by praising peace and friendship and not allowing people to come. It rather surprises me now that this had an effect. The police called on my friend in Prague and asked her who I was, and why I wanted to come. I was sorry when I heard about this, but it seems she was able to satisfy them, for I got my visa.

"The journey by train through post-war Europe went at a snail's pace. There were endless customs examinations at the border of every occupied zone, and passport and currency checks between times. Once everyone had to get out of the train while the seat cushions were turned up and the racks searched. In addition to this cause of slowness, the long-unrepaired tracks had become dangerous, and the train stopped frequently and crept on slowly. The stations were empty of anything to eat or buy, and all the glass shattered.

"But as soon as the train crossed the border into Czechoslovakia, I heard people begin to sing."

This was Dora's first encounter with a Communist state and she saw much which gave her pause for thought – lip-service to Stalin, who alone could prevent western powers subverting Communism, but also an astonishing demonstration:

"A few days after my arrival there was the grand march-past of the Sokol. I had a position of vantage – in an upper floor window looking right up Wenceslas Square. As the ranks of marchers came down towards this end of the square they started chanting 'We want Beneš' [former Prime Minister opposed to Soviet influence] and suddenly unrolled and held up American and British flags. It was like an electric shock. The woman who was sitting next to me grasped my arm and whispered over and over again: 'This is the true voice of the Czech people'."

People she met invited her to visit them: but mysteriously the plans evaporated. She had asked one boy to take her to the arms factory at Pilsen. He said they were on holiday and offered a visit to the brewery instead. In Brno a boy who had offered to take her into the mountains suddenly cried off (she thought he must have been warned off) and left her to travel alone, allowing her to have her first experience of a peasant country, and of high mountains. She found hardly anyone who could speak English, and had bad experiences of trying to use German, even in border areas where most of the older people spoke it. She had a sobering insight into the aftermath of the war:

> "Near the border I went into some houses from which Jews had been deported. Everything was in confusion, but nothing had been looted. The Czechs would not touch them. I saw wood and paper laid ready in the stove to light the fire, kitchen utensils and china, sewing machines and clothing, all worth a lot in the poverty of the country, but just falling into decay. They must have remained like that, even to the firewood in the stove, for at least five years. My friend in Prague told me she could have had a house in that area for nothing, if she would take it, but nobody would live there."

Far from being disillusioned with Communism, Dora felt this experience deepened her understanding that the class struggle was bound to sharpen after a revolution, that many things would happen that people would not understand, and that "to worry about a small degree of over-caution, or the loss of small liberties, was to be like a child, who might cry because toys were broken in a life and death struggle between adults, which he could not understand".

There was work to be done: and the Party decided that she

should organise branches of the British-Soviet Friendship Society. Outwardly an organisation dedicated to peace, friendship and goodwill, the Society was controlled by the Party. Dora's job was to set up branches, first in the South West and then further afield, and to find speakers, hold meetings and do publicity. As she was unpaid, except for travelling expenses, she took seasonal agricultural work, enjoying the company of the East Enders down for the hop-picking season in Kent.

In the General Election of 1950, the Communist Party in Devon felt confident enough to put up a candidate for the Totnes area. A report, in the form of a cyclostyled pamphlet, makes honourable mention of Dora's contribution to the campaign:

> "Amongst other comrades who shared the honour of platform work [was] Dora Scarlett ... I was particularly struck with Dora Scarlett's speech at Hennock when she showed in a constructive manner with historical illustration why we Communists are friends of the Soviet Union. The reception she got was proof enough how wrong it is to be defensive or evasive about the Soviet Union, only to finish up with questions about 'the brides', 'forced labour', or other red herrings."

(from *Our fight in the Totnes Division* – the story of the Devon and Cornwall Communist Party's first Parliamentary contest by Dave Goodman.)

Goodman evidently relishes the moment when, as the candidate was giving his speech, a Tory dame asked him, "And where do you work?" and after his reply a wag in the audience remarked, "'Er as asked that question never did no work."

The candidate got 423 votes which was noted as the "best in the country".

In late 1950, Dora's mother died. They had been living together in an old cottage in Lamberhurst, near Tunbridge Wells. She writes little about her life with her mother, but in a letter to her adopted brother Frank a touching memory surfaces:

"I have a happy memory of Mother's last day at Tunbridge Wells. She was working up to the day before her death. When I came home from work there was a cheerful fire and a tasty supper. She said, 'Look in the other room and you will see something beautiful.' It was a large bunch of yellow narcissus, which had been brought by a visitor. The next afternoon she was taken ill through the heart trouble which had affected her for 10 years, and she died within an hour or so. The narcissus were placed in her coffin. I often think of her like this."

Following her mother's death Dora continued in the old cottage, where she lived very contentedly:

"It cost six shillings a week, but the water had to be fetched from a spring a hundred yards up the road, and of course there was no gas or electricity. I whitewashed the walls, painted the furniture yellow and grey, and got one of those incandescent lamps known as a Tilly. I still remember its beauty, and the calm golden radiance of the lamp, against the background of autumn woods."

This period was a time of learning and development for Dora, now in her early forties. She loved calling meetings and being able to influence people's thoughts and lives. She enjoyed having the power to make things happen. She also developed her writing skills:

"I had always been able to write clearly and effectively, but I now learned a lot about writing good letters, how to approach others who did not know me, how to be business-like, yet to show some personal warmth, how to be persuasive. I learned the nature of secretaryship and chairmanship – the latter being a subject very little known even to many of those who take it on. I realised that good or bad chairmanship could make or mar a meeting, and that meetings did not run themselves after the speaker had mounted the platform with the audience in front of him."

There were, however, many criticisms of the Soviet Union during this period of the Cold War. The restrictions on travel, the ugly rumours of forced labour camps, and the treatment of Jews had to be dismissed: despite feeling uncomfortable about them,

"... I, and many like me, could not give up our esteem of the Soviet Union because the actions of the Soviet authorities occasionally seemed arbitrary and inscrutable. The revolution, the war, the invasion, the recovery and the final victory were matters too vast to admit of doubt because of a few pinpricks."

But doubt was seeping in, and Dora admitted there had to be some dishonesty in her responses to criticisms of the Soviet Union. "And I now realise that one must pay for dishonesty in the end."

Dora went to meetings of the World Peace Council in Paris and Vienna. She recalls the "excitement, verve and joy" of these meetings, of shaking hands with Paul Robeson, and marching behind the banner of the dove drawn by Picasso. She felt keenly

"... the innocence, the hopefulness, the kindly comradeship of these people ... There was a special flavour about it, because they still had their dreams of a better world after the war. It is impossible now, so late in the century, after the fall of Stalin's image, after Viet Nam, and in conditions of comparative affluence which has not brought happiness, to recapture that mood."

The British-Soviet Friendship Society sent her as a delegate to the first meeting of the German-Soviet Friendship Society meeting in East Berlin:

"I had never imagined anything like the devastation of Berlin. It was possible to stand looking across Friedrichstrasse and not see a single building whole and standing. Getting about involved picking a way through mounds of rubble. Demolition squads were working. Over the Brandenburg Gate the bronze horses leaned drunkenly to one side, with a red flag planted above them. The famous Adlon Hotel, where we were lodged, had no hot water, and there were large cracks in the walls. People could be seen at the breakfast tables with their own little pots of jam or butter which they had somehow acquired to supplement the hotel fare; they handled these like treasures. I found that many Berliners had been told during the war that London had been knocked flatter than Berlin and they still believed it.

"But whatever the shortages suffered by the German people, we, the delegates, were treated well and fed lavishly. I was at a reception where we had wines and spirits, caviar, various kinds of cheese and savouries, ices and good coffee. The atmosphere was what I should have called bourgeois, certainly not proletarian. It was like any

Embassy reception. I remarked on this to a German companion, and was told: 'Almost all the people you see here were in prison or concentration camp up till a few years ago. Now they are on top. Can you grudge it to them?'"

This experience made a lasting impression: "I think it was then that the feeling of Eastern Europe first really took hold of me – the feeling of limitless suffering, which made life in Western Europe, in spite of war damage and loss there, seem easy and trivial." There had been reports of the Soviet Union using forced labour in the uranium mines of Saxony; to deal with this, Dora was sent by the party to a conference in Berlin and asked to find out the truth. "I might as well have been asked to go and find out what was on the other side of the moon." Despite a brave attempt, her mission was naturally unsuccessful, and she determined never again to be so naïve and trusting when undertaking political work.

The next great opportunity arose for her in 1951 – a visit to the Soviet Union, as a member of a twenty-strong delegation of the Society for Cultural Relations with the Soviet Union. Made up mostly of "intelligentsia", the delegates were asked what they would like to see: Dora's request to stay on a collective farm was refused. But her suggested visit to one of the Central Asian republics was allowed, and Uzbekistan was chosen.

"How can I describe the delight of those three weeks? The whole of the time was crammed with interest, pleasure and wonder. Looking back, I find it somehow endearing that all was not perfectly organised, and some absurd things were done. We were lodged in the old Hotel National, which has been superseded by more modern hotels, but was pleasant enough, and looked over to the

Kremlin, and the Red Square, where the never-diminishing line of people waited every day to file through Lenin's tomb.

"Ralph Parker, the British journalist who had been living for some years in Moscow, came to see us, and I remember one of his remarks: 'The Russians are a motherly people'. I found so many little unrehearsed kindnesses, and so many helpful touches, for example, the rather plain women who sat on each floor of the hotel and would do anything for you, even to darning your clothes. I felt somehow that there was an immense reservoir of homely goodness among the common people."

Persistently plied with food and wine by their hosts, Dora, ever prudent, found a trick to avoid the endless alcohol by asking the waiters to fill her glass with black tea, which could be mistaken for wine. They spent hours in art galleries and looking at Stalin's birthday presents, then were taken to Leningrad which Dora found "entrancing". It was however Uzbekistan which was the highlight of the trip.

"Our plane flew low over thousands of miles of country so that we could see the farms and the long shelter belts of trees planted to change the climate – they zig-zagged away to the dim horizon. From the air the marks of shell holes made during the war were clearly visible although they had long been ploughed over. After stopping at Akhtubinsk we passed into Asia, and saw, far to the South and merging with the white clouds, the dazzling salt flats of the Aral Sea. Then the vast Desert of Red Sand, the Kyzyl Kum, blown into waves and furrows by the wind. At Tashkent the beginning of the irrigated land, seen from the air, was a sharp line, like a pen outline on a map.

Within this line the earth teemed with riches, grapes, melons, pomegranates, cotton, and flocks of numberless sheep which made the evening air dusty with their homecoming, just as the cows do in India. Tashkent was a modern city with trams and a department store, set among many groups of thatched clay houses. There were two very distinct sections of the population – fair Russians, in suits and short dresses, and Uzbeks, in striped trousers like pyjamas, and little round embroidered caps. It would be no use enquiring about the relations between these two groups. The answer would be that as both were building socialism their interests were identical, therefore they could not clash. I had received this kind of book answer before.

"The Uzbek girls also wore trousers and round caps, and they had long plaits of shining black hair. There were a few veiled women among them. Sometimes pictures showing women wearing the veil seem to make it an instrument of seduction and coquettishness. The veil as worn in Uzbekistan is far from this – it is made of horsehair, and stands away from the face and body front and back, so that unless the woman moves it is impossible to tell which way she is facing. One imagines an old woman inside this tent, but I saw a young rounded arm come out to pick up purchases in a shop. I do not know whether the veil has been completely abandoned since then. We went to an Uzbek opera in the magnificent white domed opera house; it was about the fight of women to live without the veil.

"I was not happy about the productions of art and handicraft which we saw. I was convinced that a people like the Uzbeks must have some very fine handicraft. The art gallery was full of 'Socialist realism' expressed in such pictures as 'Share-out day on the collective farm'. The department store had little to buy of artistic interest except round embroidered caps and the china had some dimly traditional designs but was of poor quality. At the Stalin Cotton Mill, said to be the largest in the Soviet Union, we were each invited to choose a piece of dress material for ourselves. The designs were like those of the cheaper products of Lancashire, and after looking vainly for something reflecting local art, I took a plain emerald green piece."

Some photographs have survived of this trip: Dora with a fixed polite smile looking at a display of Stalin's birthday presents, or inspecting state construction projects, and in contrast a relaxed and happy Dora in Tashkent with her arms around a group of Uzbek women in the sunshine.

Dora (seated third from left) in Tashkent

Chapter 5

RADIO BUDAPEST AND THE UPRISING

Aspirations drowned in blood.

At the end of 1952 Dora, now 47, was invited to work in the foreign language section of an Eastern European radio station. She jumped at the chance. The party chose to send her to Budapest: "I could not know it at the time, but this was an extremely momentous decision – probably the most far-reaching in my life." Before she left, she was told it was a secret assignment, and she must change her rather distinctive surname to the more anonymous "Walton". Further, she had to take a Hungarian name as she was supposed to be a Hungarian broadcaster, speaking in English to English audiences. Despite her lack of broadcasting experience, she found that "literary accomplishments or journalistic experience were of secondary account compared with political rectitude". Her discovery of Hungary began.

"I first saw Budapest through a flurry of snow, in February, 1953. It seemed a grey and shabby city, with unrepaired war damage still showing on many of the buildings, with screeching trams and muffled-up inhabitants. But it was a comfortably small city; it was easy to see the edges of it, and the white and black half-frozen Danube flowed through the heart of it, crossed by the Széchenyi Chain Bridge. Beyond rose the Gellert Hill, crowned by the Liberation Memorial, a young girl holding up a palm branch with both hands. A little farther upstream was the long outline of the old fortress city of

Buda. To me there has always been something very memorable in this view of the city, and I think many others who have known it have felt the same.

"The new block of flats which was being specially built for radio workers was not completed, so I was lodged in the Gellert Hotel, which is built over one of those thermal springs which spout out in so many places from the soil of Budapest. There was constant very hot water, a warm indoor swimming pool and an outdoor bath. Most of the people of Budapest were then shivering round inadequately fuelled stoves, or going to espresso cafes to keep warm, making a small cup of black coffee last for an hour or so. The dining room of the Gellert was ornamented with gilding and potted palms; the waiters were attentive and the cutlery massive. This was very unlike what I expected in a 'People's Democracy', but I had no choice in the matter. My fellow guests were not the affluent tourists for whom the hotel had been built in pre-war days. I think that many were people on minor business missions from other East European countries or other parts of Hungary. Soviet visitors, or Party officials, had special hotels and special holiday resorts."

Dora was amused to find that English listeners to her broadcasts really thought she was Hungarian, and would send her pictures of England and tales of their life there. One man actually wrote from the street where she was born, but of course she could not give away her real identity. This subterfuge caused her some misgivings. She had a pleasant flat in a new block in the diplomatic quarter and lived there until November 1956. It was, she felt a "divided life", one part giving pleasure, and one "full of disappointment, frustration and doubt."

Soviet policy and speeches made up the bulk of her broadcasts. This was the rule, and all other topics were subordinate to this.

"But provided we did our duty by relaying the right news and speeches, we were allowed some latitude in the presentation of other matters. Culture was important. ... The country, lying at the crossroads of many European trade routes even before the dawn of history, is very rich in prehistoric and Roman remains, Turkish baths and mosques, and Baroque churches. It also hasa living folk art in costume, dance and music. It was quite in order in the Radio to write, as I did, a series of 'Pages from Hungarian History', or a history of Hungarian music, illustrated by records which I took the greatest pleasure in discovering in the Radio music library. Among these was an actual recording made by Bartok during his researches in the villages; it gave the quavering voices of old people singing in a style soon to be forgotten. I also wrote about vintages, the wine cellars of Tokay, Danube steamers, markets, the stalactite caves of Aggtelek, Hungarian cooking, holidays, the opera, the Pioneer railway – a real railway run by children in the Buda Hills – the making of salami and fine china. On such subjects I collected my own material, but we were also offered very frequent chances of going out in the Radio van to report on factories, farms and various public institutions; we were able to be present at the opening of parliament and every other state occasion. When we went out with the Radio, we usually met the Party Secretary of the place, and received the official figures; we were able to ask questions and make interviews with selected workers. On the whole, the information given me was correct as far as it went, but, as I came to realise little by little, there was a lot going on which could not be mentioned."

The English section came in for frequent criticism from the more militant French and Italian sections. It was felt they had lost sight of the fact that their purpose was not information or entertainment but to prepare for revolution. Dora became increasingly aware of the political tensions and the lack of any freedom of speech and saw how in the face of intolerable pressure people were forced to have both a public and a private face.

The effect of the constantly changing political fortunes of leaders such as Lásló Rajk, a minister in 1949 condemned and executed on the charge of being a supporter of Tito, then rehabilitated in 1956, and Imre Nagy, "the liberalising Prime Minister who was put in to save the situation when the country had been driven to the brink of economic ruin by the excessive pace of the Five Year Plan" who was ousted from power in 1955, was recounted by Tibor Déry in a book Dora encouraged me to read called *Nikki*. This heart-breaking story of a little dog and its owners shows ordinary people deeply affected, and ultimately destroyed, by the volatile political situation in Hungary. Sometimes the only response was a joke:

"A story was circulated of two men who found themselves together in prison. 'What are you in for?' asks one. 'For supporting Imre Nagy.' 'What are you in for?' 'For opposing Imre Nagy' replies the other. They both turn to a third man who has not yet spoken – 'And you?' 'I'm Imre Nagy', he answers.

"In my book, *Window onto Hungary* I gave a very detailed and documented account of what I found to be the actual state of affairs When I wrote about the present,

53

I tended to write of country life and nature, shipping on the Danube, folk art, and innocuous events like exhibitions, concerts, and operatic performances, for which one could give musical excerpts. I scarcely ever stood up to speak at meetings, as I found it impossible to say anything which would be acceptable and at the same time sincere."

She seriously thought of resigning.

"I stayed on partly because I had begun to feel I had roots in the country, and partly because Hungarian friends told me many times that I should stay. They had begun to say that there would soon be changes in the political situation, and by 1955 there were indeed signs that something would happen. They said, too, that the country needed all its friends, and those who really knew what Hungarians suffered would be able to tell it to the outside world. They were more right than they knew. I would have been extremely sorry if I had left before the uprising of 1956, and had lost my chance to be an eyewitness. I have no regrets that I decided to stay."

Her faith, however, in the party was being undermined:

"To me it seems the worst indictment of the methods of the Party was that they corrupted those who were its wholehearted followers, and who were not moved by greed or ambition. There were people who really believed that what was happening in Hungary was part of the world proletarian revolution (as it had been my belief when I went there) and for this they were ready to lay down their lives. They were likewise ready to lie, and falsify evidence, and betray their friends."

Dora used her free time to explore widely, and there is an obvious relish in her accounts of taking the tram to the railhead, travelling into the countryside and walking all day, sometimes returning on a paddle steamer down the Danube. She visited "towns full of peasants in greasy sheepskin coats and women in rusty black." She spent her longer holidays in Workers' Holiday Homes, and saw more of the country.

"The Great Plain seems endless; unfenced strips of wheat, maize, sunflowers follow one another, broken by small vineyards; lines of soaring poplars, and waste land grazed by flocks of white geese. I used to think that there must be more geese than people in Hungary, and this was probably true. Every peasant family kept its can of goose grease for the winter, and its mountainous feather beds of goose down. Ox carts creak along the roads, and in the villages old men in collarless shirts sit on benches in the evening, smoking long pipes. Often a cart would be carrying a whole family to a wedding or other festivity; the men would be in black, but the girls in full skirts, as bright as a garden of flowers. Two rivers, the Danube and the Tisza, cross this plain, winding slowly, with many sandy, willow-fringed islands."

The travelling was not without its hardships: few shops, scarce food and little comfort; but she found the peasants were better off than city dwellers:

"When I visited them in their homes, I had goulash of beef or pork, chicken soup (unrefined, with head and feet all in, but rich) hunks of nutty rye bread, fat bacon, fresh green peppers, and home-made wine. A peasant society is the toughest in the world.

"My appreciation of the Hungarian peasant was by no means a sentimental love of the country. I began to see here again, though dimly, a reflection of my earlier ideal of the Distributist society, an ideal abandoned in favour of Marxism, only because I had seen no means of achieving it. It had been the contention of the Distributists that a society in which a producer owned the means of production as the normal condition of affairs – not as a collective but as a person – would be the freest society possible, and the best able to stand against coercion and tyranny."

Imre Nagy's reforms were designed to give the peasants more power over their own affairs; when he was turned out of office, his reforms were reversed. Meat disappeared from the Budapest shops, and Dora realised the peasants were on strike, killing their pigs for themselves and refusing to send meat to market. This was the beginning of a very turbulent and momentous period. She writes with thoroughness, keen understanding and real sympathy for the workers and peasants suffering under what became increasingly an incompetent and invalid government. The removal of Nagy proved a decisive moment for Dora:

"[I]t was a turning point for me, because I saw clearly, once and for all, that what was happening in Hungary had nothing at all to do with Marxism, with the working-class struggle, or world revolution. It had to do with power, and not people's power, but the power of megalomaniac individuals like Stalin and his best disciple, Ràkosi, or faceless, unseen and unapproachable bodies like the AVO [the secret police]. The rest of my time in Hungary was spent watching the signs that this power was crumbling, and then, at the end, seeing it return again."

The first sign of what was to come was the inexplicable omission of any broadcast of Krushchev's momentous speech at the 20th Congress of the Communist Party in February 1955. Dora only saw a copy which had been dropped from a propaganda balloon from West Germany. The celebration of Stalin's birthday in December of the same year had also gone unreported. Unrest began to grow, and Dora felt they were living in a kind of "hopeful dream".

> "After eight years of living as nonentities ordinary people began to find, to their surprise, that they really counted for something; that they could speak their minds and do their work and (they thought) influence the future of their country. This gave rise to a state of euphoria, in which many sincere people believed it would be possible to undo the 'mistakes' and excesses of Stalinism and build a Hungary truly socialist, truly Hungarian, and at peace with East and West. This dream, like the mirages sometimes seen on the Hortobágy, the arid plain of Eastern Hungary, was something impossible to reach. It was not based on the realities of international politics; it could not stand the brutal force of the cold war. Those who believed in such a simple, human, kindly and sensible solution had to be crushed between the millstones of east and west, and their aspirations drowned in blood."

As dissent grew, Dora was impressed at the way writers used innocuous means to send hidden messages and was especially moved when she gate-crashed a performance of an opera by Kodály. Although originally a play about Turkish domination of Hungary in the 16th and 17th centuries, the piece, without a word altered, could be transposed into the twentieth century, and the recurring refrain, "Let the Hungarians alone!" was taken up and echoed around the hall. Kodály himself was brought to the stage to receive fifteen minutes of applause.

Party officials who were present sat stony-faced and left before the end of the cheering. People's appetite for freedom of expression, long suppressed, began to show: two thousand people attended a meeting of dissident writers, the overflow crowd standing in the rain, and Mrs. Rajk, widow of the unjustly executed minister, made an impassioned speech against Rákosi, who was now out of favour. Control of the Press slipped, and a *Monday Newspaper* came out: the simple fact of its publication and massive sales saying more than the articles it contained.

Dora was sent to report on a student demonstration on October 23rd:

> "It was a warm afternoon, and so little did I foresee what would happen that I left my coat and scarf in the office, and my keys and pen on my desk thinking I should be back by five o'clock. I did not set foot in the Radio again for a week. When I did, I found the office in exactly the same state as it had been left, except that one window had been broken by a bullet and there was splintered glass on the floor."

They joined the march which passed through the most important streets in the city, singing the Internationale and the Marseillaise:

"At one point I saw a little old woman standing, trembling and hesitant, on the kerb. She was short, frail as a sparrow, with sharp nose and chin, and indrawn cheeks. I thought that perhaps she wanted to cross the road, and was afraid of the crowd, but just as I was about to offer help, she drew herself up, raised her hands above her head and her thin voice rose above the hubbub in; *Eljen*! – 'Long live!' ... Her eyes, of the milky pale blue of age, were alight with joy. In a moment I had passed her, drawn along by the crowd, but her face remained with me as a clear, sharp image, and I sometimes wondered in the weeks that followed, whether she survived, or whether she had to mourn a son or grandson killed in the fighting. She seemed a symbol of the many, many old people in Budapest who had suffered so much during long years, and were now kindled by the hope and enthusiasm of the youth in these October days."

The demonstrators stood before the parliament building, singing the National Anthem, holding flags from which the centre, with its hated coat of arms, had been cut out, and shouting their demands, including the return of Imre Nagy. At one point all the street lights were put out, and people lit rolled- up newspapers, which allowed Dora to see for herself the vast size of the crowd, the sky all around red from the burning torches. An official shouted from a balcony that Imre Nagy had been sent for; someone told Dora the Radio offices were in the hands of the AVO and a group set off in a lorry to liberate them. Imre Nagy appeared and made a short speech but, "by coming he had signed his death warrant."

On her way to the Radio offices Dora heard shots and found an AVO van overturned and in flames, and an unarmed crowd, confronting army lorries full of troops. Tear gas stung her eyes. It appeared a delegation of demonstrators had entered the Radio offices intending to broadcast their demands. These delegates had not reappeared and there were fears for their safety at the hands of the AVO. Feeling against the AVO was very strong: Dora heard from colleagues who had stayed in the building, hiding from the firing, that at one point three AVO men tried to take refuge but were found by the insurgents and killed. After midnight Dora saw the first groups of young men with rifles, and saw cars on fire. The Russian bookshops were ransacked and all the books burned; hastily produced newssheets were handed round in support of the revolution; armed police appeared.

"I turned homewards down Mayakovsky Street. Until this moment I had not noticed that I was tired, nor had it once occurred to me to feel frightened. I had been out for twelve hours without once stopping to rest or having a bite to eat; I was scarcely conscious of myself at all. In the darkness of Mayakovsky Street flags were hanging from the house windows, and I could make out that each one had a circular hole, where the coat of arms was cut away. I did not know till next day that the statue of Stalin had actually been taken down. This entailed much effort, as well as the bringing of tools from the factories. The boots were left standing on the pedestal and someone stuck a Hungarian flag in them. What I did know was that among all the thousands of people I had listened to, spoken to, or jostled against, I heard not one expression of hostility to what was being done, or even mild disapproval of it. I went to bed about three o'clock, and at five I was awakened by the roar of tanks passing outside my window."

The tanks were Soviet tanks sent from Western Hungary. They were attacked in ad hoc fashion with small arms and petrol bombs, but could not manoeuvre round the narrow streets, into which their attackers fled. They were sent to protect Soviet buildings and personnel. It was impossible for Dora to get to the Radio offices and it was very unclear what messages they should broadcast even if they could; meetings of colleagues were held in her block of flats but no broadcasts could be made.

What shocked her most of all was the complete collapse of the Party – split into various unequal factions, some supporters of the uprising, some influential political thinkers, some informers and spies, and some functionaries, it could not hold: "a Party of nine thousand members had vanished overnight".

"During the big demonstration in front of Parliament there had been a sudden volley of fire. It will never be known exactly how many died, because the bodies were dumped in the Danube, but most estimates gave a hundred, and more likely two hundred. In the confusion no one was really certain who fired, but the belief of most people who were near the spot – and I spoke to many of them in an effort to get at the truth – was that the AVO fired, and the Russian troops tried to protect the crowd. At the moment, when there had been so many desertions from the Soviet forces, popular feeling towards the Russians was growing more friendly, and so people were more ready to believe it was the AVO who had fired.

"Anger against the AVO rose higher and higher. Pay slips were found in the pockets of some of the AVO men; they were getting nine thousand Forints a month, while the average wage was one thousand, and unskilled workers got six to eight hundred. The pay slips were pinned to the bodies for all to see. At times you would see a small crowd of people standing at some road crossing, looking at a battered and overturned car. They did not want to talk much, and they offered no explanations or justifications. They would just say 'AVO'. They stood in silence. It was a remarkable fact that in a city where private cars were unobtainable by the ordinary public, and in an insurrection in which transport was badly needed, so many AVO cars were put out of action. No one would take them."

Newspapers became vital for dissemination of information, and new ones sprang up. People were hungry for the free printed word. Dora collected many of these papers, admiring their "frankness, clarity and enthusiasm":

"Their tone was proud and jubilant, without any sign of hysteria; they called for order, national unity, and defence to the utmost of all gains of the revolution. Some are only single sheets, and some only four pages, but they thought it worth the space to print poems – some old ones, like Petőfi's famous: 'The sea has risen, the sea of the peoples' or new ones hammered out in the stress of the uprising. The Police paper recalled proudly how groups of police joined the demonstrators on the 23rd, and how none raised a weapon against the insurgents: 'From the first moment the Budapest Police knew where their place was'."

But where was the Radio in all this? No foreign language broadcasts were being made, only the Home Service was on the air. One sports commentator made an ill-judged remark about the demonstrators being looters, prompting fierce indignation:

"There stood the Russian bookshop, gaping and empty, with the mountain of black ashes from its books still smouldering in the street. This was a political protest – no one wanted the books. Just across the way was an antique shop, full of exquisite china and ivory, quite untouched. There were broken windows through which I could have easily put my hand to take out a blouse or a pair of shoes; a baby's pram (an expensive treasure) stood in a little showcase from which all the glass had fallen out.

An old lady looked at some cakes in a broken window, and said she would take them out and use them before they spoiled. The passers-by would not allow it; better let a few cakes spoil than set an example which might look like looting. When at last the goods in the windows of the department stores began to get dusty and damaged, they were taken out and replaced by a notice saying: 'All goods are safe in the store room; we Hungarians do not loot'."

The Radio was becoming more and more unpopular, and completely out of step with popular feeling. The political leaders of the Foreign Language department simply disappeared: so the journalists had no supervision and no work. The Revolutionary Council was broadcasting from Parliament.

Food and news were two essentials, and these, now export of food had been stopped, could be obtained at the same time:

"There were mountains of chickens and ducks in the biggest market, beautifully trussed and wrapped in greaseproof paper bearing the stamp of the export agency, Terimpex. For the first time in Hungary I could buy good meat easily. But owing to transport difficulties the supplies were concentrated in a few state shops and large covered markets. This meant it was necessary to stand in line for an hour or two, but the market was one of the best places in which to keep an ear to the ground and feel the movements of public opinion.

"At other times there would have been grumbling, but now everyone was remarkably patient and good-natured. I heard no word of condemnation of the rising, and the insurgents were always spoken of as 'ours'."

The streets were full of posters, walls and shop windows

plastered with articles, cartoons and jokes. Anyone could put anything up, and the overwhelming message was democratisation, withdrawal of Soviet troops, treatment of Hungary as an independent country, elections with more than one party, and the disbanding of the AVO. "Russians go home" was also widespread. Dora saw in all these slogans nothing but justice and common sense.

Attending meetings of the Revolutionary Council, Dora was impressed by the efficiency and clarity of the meetings, in contrast to the dreary hours she had sat through in previous years. The position of the foreign language service was not yet clear.

On October 30th the tanks began to leave Budapest.

"Down by the Danube embankment, in the foggy dusk, I watched the field guns and the long lines of ammunition lorries rumbling by. The continuous roar of tanks echoed through the deserted streets. In the former Stalin Avenue I stood looking at lines of trucks, each drawing a field kitchen, each with a little bright fire glowing below, and steam puffing gaily from the top."

A couple of days later on November 1st, Dora is walking through the main streets after dusk:

"I saw candles appearing in many windows. For a moment I thought the electricity had failed, but then I noticed the street lighting was still on. I remembered the date; it was the eve of All Souls' Day, the day of remembrance for the dead. More and more candles began to glow, on window ledges, in front of street corner shrines, and in churches, where vast numbers of people were coming and going, and kneeling in prayer. In the city there were new graves in every little grassy space; fighters had been buried where they fell, partly as a public gesture and partly because it was impossible to have a regular funeral while the fighting continued. These graves were lit by candles, marked by rough wooden crosses, and hand-written inscriptions. Crowds stood by them. I was seeing a city in mourning, but in a mood of solemn exaltation, too."

There were, however, rumours that this was not a complete withdrawal. Dora suspected the Russians were regrouping, and feared a second attack. While the insurgents freed thousands of political prisoners, and Budapest began to return to normal, there continued to be news of Soviet troop movements, and a ring of steel appeared to be surrounding the city. Despite this atmosphere of foreboding, Dora was offered a return to her job at the Radio, where she would be allowed to be freer and more objective. She readily agreed. A meeting was set for the next day, November 4th.

"My last thought as I fell asleep that night was of what I intended to say at the meeting. At five o'clock in the morning I was awakened by the distant sound of heavy gunfire. I switched on the radio, and I heard the National Anthem and the Szózat [the 'second National Anthem of Hungary']. Then the voice of Imre Nagy said: 'At dawn today the Soviet forces made an unprovoked attack on the capital, with the obvious intention of overthrowing the lawful democratic Hungarian Government. Our troops are resisting; the Government is in its place. This is my message to Hungary and to the world'. This was repeated in English and German. Just before seven the Writers' Association broadcast an appeal to all writers, scientists

65

and leaders of intellectual life in all countries to take their cause to heart. Then the radio was silent. The gunfire came steadily nearer."

And so the final episode of Dora's life in Hungary began. Trapped for three days in her apartment, hearing fierce fighting all around, it was not until the radio came on again that she discovered a political leader called Kadar had formed a new government based outside Budapest and was on the Russians' side. Much to Dora's disgust, his radio station was playing light popular music:

"'Budapest, Budapest! What a proud and beautiful city you are! How life throbs in your streets!' This, coming at a moment when Budapest was fighting for its life, and the streets were littered with corpses, seemed unbearable effrontery, and confirmed my belief that those who sell their consciences lose their good taste and sense of decency too."

Trudging through streets full of broken glass, past shattered buildings and new graves, unable to buy food or go to work, with an administration no longer functioning, and with a residence permit about to expire, Dora had to make a decision:

"I could have pleaded that I felt unable to work in the Radio after the shocks of recent days, but this was not true. I wanted to stay and see what would happen. Moreover, although I could have been sent back to England, with my fare paid, in good standing with the Communist Party, and as having fulfilled my time in Hungary, this could not be done at such short notice. I would be asked to stay on until the depleted staff could be made up. And the first days back in the Radio would be the decisive ones, when we should have to tell the world what had happened."

After some thought, she went to the British Legation, and was offered a place in the next lorry convoy out of the country. Having written a letter of resignation to the Radio, she could find no one to give it to and simply left it on her desk. Leaving everything behind in her flat, placing her spare Hungarian forints in one of the many open suitcases collecting in the street for bereaved families, she left on the 15th November with seventeen other people, holders of British or Dominion passports, on a heart-breaking journey to the Austrian border.

"The morning was damp and grey. The flags still hung on the buildings bedraggled by three weeks of weather, still brave, defiant and pathetic. We passed through the mining town of Dorog, where the entire population seemed to be out in the streets. The pits were on strike. In a field an old peasant took off his high fur hat and bowed with grave dignity. I felt I did not deserve this. What had I done that I should be riding safely in comparative comfort while so many were trudging the wet roads or staying behind to face failure and bitterness, and perhaps savage reprisals?"

At the British Embassy in Vienna they were fed, put in hotels, and given rail tickets for their journey home.

The Christmas lights of Oxford Street did nothing to cheer Dora on her return, suffering from an extreme case of what she calls "refugee sickness". The plethora of tawdry, useless goods on sale after the austerity of Hungary oppressed her. Working as a counter assistant in a West End shop, selling calendars, Dora's spirits were at a low ebb:

"My feet ached, but my heart ached much more. In spirit I was walking down dark streets, past shattered houses, and seeing the torn and bedraggled flags. Why, when so much that was tragic, terrible and beautiful was happening in the world, could artists not design something better than eighteenth century coaches in snow, or cottages among hollyhocks?"

There was little anyone could do to help. "The refugee's need is for others to share, fully and in all detail the knowledge of what has happened, and this, of course, is impossible."

Amongst Dora's papers is the story of Edith Bone. Edith Bone was Hungarian by birth but had a British passport and had been living in London. She was a staunch Communist, nicknamed "The Battleaxe". She and Dora had both attended the Paris Peace Congress in 1949, and Edith went on to Hungary. When Dora was in the Soviet Union the following year, as a delegate of the Society for Cultural Relations, she was surprised to see a newspaper headline asking "Where is Edith Bone?" It seemed that she had not returned from the trip to Hungary and had disappeared. Nothing more was heard until Dora, when she took refuge in the British Legation, was told, "Guess who has been here before you – Edith Bone! She is now well on her way to England." Dora sought out Edith Bone on her return and heard the full story. As she tried to leave Hungary, Edith Bone had been arrested. She had been imprisoned, in solitary confinement, without trial, in the AVO headquarters just a block away from Dora's apartment in Budapest. She had no idea that the uprising was taking place until a group of young men with rifles burst into her cell and said "Run, run for your life!" Musing on this story, Dora reflects: "I do not know how far the cellars of the AVO extended, but in those years between 1953 and 1956 I was so close to her that I might have actually been walking above her head ... [Had] those young men with rifles not burst through the doors she would probably have never come out alive."

When Dora visited Bone, living contentedly in her cottage in Sussex, she marvelled at the strength of character she must have had to survive those years of imprisonment. Bone chose to give her story to the *Daily Express* under the heading "I suffered and I accuse". The *Daily Worker* would not publish it, and this was the treatment Dora also received: the Communist Party did not want to hear what she had to say.

Alison Selford, who had been television critic for the *Daily Worker*, wrote about meeting Dora for the first time in her book, *The Death of Uncle Joe*, which graphically describes the turmoil in the British Communist Party over the events in Hungary:

"When she came to see us, Dora described her conversation with John Gollan [leader of the Communist Party]. She told him all about the Communist bosses, their privileged beach behind barbed wire on Lake Balaton, the long record of arrests, frame- ups, tortures and executions, and the final explosion of popular hatred against the security policemen ... Gollan heard her out and said in his gentle Edinburgh voice, 'Och, I wish we'd known a' this'. He then continued to speak and write as if he did not know it."

The Communist Party of Great Britain wanted to justify the Soviet intervention, but Dora, like many members, did not agree. She had lost faith. She wrote: "What sort of international party is it, if the national leaders are kept in such ignorance?" Alison shows quite clearly how they chose to remain in ignorance, and even suppress information, in order to hold the Party line.

In a letter to Alison, Dora wrote:

> "My experiences since returning from Hungary could have been more help to the struggle for inner-Party democracy if only I had realised earlier that such a struggle was going on, and that the forces on this side within the Party were quite strong. But I had been quite isolated from British party life, and I had a struggle in my own mind, which had been going on long before the rising in Hungary, to decide whether the evils I saw around me were the result of the very nature of the party or whether they were 'mistakes' which would ultimately be rectified. The rising was for me not a decisive point; I had reached that point earlier. My attitude when I came back was therefore too individualistic. My chief concern was the tell the Party what I had experienced, and to resign."

Several authors rushed out books and booklets commenting on the events in Hungary: Charlie Coutts's "sixpenny pamphlet", *Eye Witness in Hungary*, came in for particular criticism from Dora in a scathing review in *The Tribune*, January 25th, 1957, entitled, indignantly, *I was in Hungary too, Mr Coutts*. Drawing on her own experiences she rebuts many of his conclusions, especially his opinion that without Soviet interference the revolution in Hungary would have turned into a prolonged civil war.

Dora knew she had enough material for a book, but when she approached Gollancz, they said that by the time she had written it the world would have moved on and no one would be interested. In the end she was encouraged by her friend Ralph

Russell, a Party member, who offered her hospitality.

Alison remembers that Dora lodged at first with a couple of CP members, but could not agree with them over Hungary: "When she tried to tell them what she had seen in Hungary they screamed, it couldn't be true; it mustn't be true."

Alison offered Dora a housekeeping job with her parents, the McLeods. The post lasted for about a year and Dora was remembered as the ideal housekeeper, dealing patiently with an old lady with dementia and enjoying intellectual conversations with Mr. McLeod. By the end of 1957 she had 73 orders for her book *Window onto Hungary*. Blackwell's said they would publish if they could guarantee American sales. In the end she got it privately published by Broadacre Books in Bradford who went out of business before fulfilling all the orders. Dora just about managed to cover her costs. It was still being read in 1974, and Dora felt it had reached those who needed it.

In his book *The Hungarian Tragedy* and other writings, the Marxist journalist Peter Fryer wrote:

"It is a sad comment on the present state of publishing in Britain, and on the real feelings about the Hungarian workers' struggles and sufferings of many of those who claimed to support their revolution in 1956, that far and away the best book yet to appear about that revolution could find no London publisher. Many of the well-printed books that came out about those events were of only ephemeral value; one at least – Noel Barber's – was tripe from beginning to end. Dora Scarlett's *Window onto Hungary*, for all the austerity of its duplicated pages, stands head and shoulders above these – indeed above any other eyewitness account of the uprising and its suppression that exists in English."

He notes that unlike most commentators on the uprising, Dora had spent three years and nine months in the country; she had not rushed into print but took time to prepare a "careful, detailed and exceedingly readable account of Hungary's history, and of economic, social and political conditions". Above all, her ability to speak Hungarian gave her a unique insight into the views of ordinary people, and in Fryer's opinion made her account of great value.

Imre Nagy and three other leaders of the uprising, one known personally to Dora, were executed in June 1958. Dora marched down Oxford Street behind placards demanding "Avenge Imre Nagy" although apart from declaring war on the Soviet Union, she had no idea how that could be achieved.

"There was not much interest among the people on the pavements. But at one point I saw a man read the placard, then slowly take off his hat, and stand so at the kerb till the procession had passed. I thanked him in my heart. On a few occasions I have seen individuals whose actions have seemed symbolic, so as to stamp them indelibly on my memory. One was the little old woman who raised her frail voice to greet the demonstrators of October 23rd. Another was this unknown man, who alone in the crowd paid tribute to Imre Nagy."

Dora's misery and feeling of dislocation went on for some time.

"By July 1959 I had done all I could to sell my book. I was without plans or prospects, and I had a feeling that life had come to an end. I had settled down to some extent; I realised that it was no use giving in to the pain and bitterness and nostalgia that surged over me whenever I was touched by some thought of Hungary. But I was still suffering from refugee sickness – the feeling that I had had an experience which I could never fully understand, and which robbed all the rest of life of its meaning ... I had been through a wild and tangled forest of political ideas, and come out into what appeared to be a barren and featureless country, but, however bleak the prospect, I knew I could not tread that path again."

Although she had lost faith in Communism, she had no faith in Capitalism either, and could find nothing to put her energies into until Ralph Russell, a real Indophile, put the idea into her head of going to India.

"It was a good and far-seeing thought. He asked me how I felt about it, and I said I had been interested in India ever since my school days, but other plans had pushed it into the background. I said I did not know what I would do in India. He said: 'You will find something'. I said I had enough money to get there, but not enough to get back. He said: 'Well, you can stay there'."

WINDOW
ONTO
HUNGARY

Dora Scarlett

The cover of Dora's book

Chapter 6

DISCOVERING INDIA

Whoso will, from pride released,
Contemning neither man nor beast,
May hear the soul of all the East...

(Rudyard Kipling)

Dora remembered having met a writer called Monica Felton. Monica had gone to India, to write a biography of Rajagopalachari ("Rajaji") a famous politician and old associate of Gandhi. She was living in Madras, (now Chennai) and invited Dora to stay; so it was on the SS *Oranje* bound for Colombo in Ceylon (now Sri Lanka) that Dora made her passage to India. Once she had arrived in India, she was never to return to England, or set foot in any other country, again.

Dora disembarked in Sri Lanka just after the assassination of the prime minister, Mrs. Bandaranaike, and was immediately drawn into the political life of Colombo for the short time she was there. She wrote an article for *The Guardian* that she suspected was seized by the authorities as it received no response. She found the mix of Ceylonese politics with religion mystifying, commenting drily, "as to why people who won't kill an insect will shoot the prime minister, the Ceylonese themselves can't tell you that."

But her delight on arriving in India was immediate: "Life here is absolutely fascinating in its beauty, its diversity and its horrors". Despite living like a memsahib with an official of the

British Council: "It irks me beyond bearing that a grown man should make my bed, and I can't bear to sit in a rickshaw and see a skinny old man bending his back and sweating to pull me along," she was soon entranced: "Half an hour wandering in any bazaar shows you the pattern of life and it's a pattern I like and feel at home with."

She spent her free time exploring Madras, the port reminding her of Liverpool's docklands, with the cart horses replaced by "mighty white or cream bullocks drawing flat carts driven by naked black-skinned men", and watching people living and sleeping on the streets, their shabby huts "astonishingly, even touchingly, clean."

Her first experience of a visit to a temple in Mylapore made a great impression:

"I had thought I knew a little about Hinduism, but I felt nothing but bewilderment. In a small, dark, unventilated chamber, worshippers were making the circuit of a large smooth stone on a pedestal. Something like an eye had been painted on it and a white cloth tied around its middle. In other places bells were ringing, and people were pressing forward to shrines, inside which lamps were blazing around figures scarcely recognisable under loads of flowers and jewels. A priest held out a plate of ashes, which the worshippers took and smeared on their foreheads. Others received some kind of liquid in the cupped hands and drank it. Still others took a few rose petals. In a quiet corner of the enclosure, all alone, a man was continually prostrating himself. There was nothing like an order of service – all seemed to follow individual inclinations."

Living in a middle-class home, in relative comfort, and dealing with servants was uncongenial; she hated being called "Madam" and waited on. She knew in order to see the real India – the "land of villages" – she would have to find a way out of the city.

"But if you set foot in an Indian village you will immediately be surrounded by a crowd and stared at as a curiosity. A mob of children (who may never have seen a white person before) will follow you everywhere; even if you have an interpreter nothing like a normal conversation will be possible; you will be quite unable to find out how people live and what goes on there. If you see the village without yourself being seen, it will be blind and dumb to you, concealing its secret life behind its crooked, sun-baked walls."

Luckily, she found some voluntary work with the Young Women's Christian Association, going in a van to a village called Mudichur where they ran a weekly clinic. Dora would sit by the doctor, writing patients' names and ailments on a card. In this way, she learned a little of the language and gained some knowledge of common medical problems. Most unexpectedly, after a few months, she was asked to go and live in the village to keep an eye on things between clinics. This was the chance she had been waiting for.

"I am not going to claim that I went into the village in any spirit of dedication or self-sacrifice. It was exploration, and it has never been any sacrifice to me to go exploring, even if the roads are long and the rocks steep. I was willing to do my best to make a success of whatever it was that I was supposed to do (the assignment was rather vague) but the main attraction was that here was a strange life to be seen, tasted, felt and, as far as might be, understood."

A letter from 1960 to Alison from Mudichur begins delightedly, "I have a little house" and despite her recognition that, "if you set foot in an Indian village with an open mind and friendly intentions it will eat you up", she knows she is on the right track. "One thing I have learned is that aid from outside is no good unless personal relationships are built in the village," but building those personal relationships is not without frustrations: "since I have been typing this letter four or five people have looked through the window and asked to come in (and been refused) ... I like to be matey but life just gets impossible."

The accounts of her early days in Mudichur are full of humour, exasperation and genuine delight. She begins by living in the spacious, airy dispensary: "But the dispensary was airy because it had windows all round, and those windows were not free from peering faces for a single moment of the day."

Coping with the unfamiliarity, the lack of privacy and the inability to speak the language was particularly trying: as she never locked the door,

"... the string cot which had been put for me was always occupied by five or six women gossiping and letting their babies crawl about. I had no privacy whatever except in a tiny dark latrine, where I had to take my bath, and I had nothing to cook on but a small electric ring. It was all very kindly intended, and I am sure the women had no idea what it means, especially to a Westerner, to be the object of curiosity for twelve hours a day; they would have been delighted if I could have sat down with them for a chat. ... These days were, without a doubt, the hardest and loneliest of my whole life.

"I thought of English villages I had known; April evenings
when the cuckoo called through orchards drenched with
showers; cottage gardens with trim hedges; Georgian
houses round the Green, and dim churches smelling of
prayer books and hassocks, with the chancel floor well-
scrubbed and the brasses polished. I remembered the
middle-class people living in modernised country houses,
with deep window seats and old beams, but new
refrigerators and washing machines; the intelligent
collections of books; the frank, fair, lively children, happy
in the country, but easily able to get into town; the
toasters and coffee percolators, the formica-topped
kitchen tables, the modern art on the walls, the car in the
garage and the family bicycles in the shed; the geyser and
the soft Turkish towels in the white bathroom."

Despite this deep nostalgia, those early days in Mudichur began
to reveal the authentic life she has been searching for:

"I could not tell at first what it was that made the Indian
village seem so significant to me. Something was there
which I must find out. It was like a message of very deep
meaning delivered in an unknown tongue. Because I went
to the village alone and unprotected, nothing could
intervene between me and this message; there were no
comments from other people, no parties of tourists, no
one bringing foreign laughter or foreign inquisitiveness.
The village was mine: if it spoke, I could listen.

"... I think my life up to this point had been a pilgrimage
in search of reality. I tried to find it in the English village,
then in Communism, then in Hungary. I believe I touched
it on that night in October 1956 when I saw Budapest in

revolt, but the clouds closed again over that brief vision. I found it in an Indian village ...

"I did not reason this out when first I went to the village. I just had a feeling that if I saw this thing through, in spite of the loneliness, and the sense of my own futility that dogged me, I should get to somewhere I wanted to be. I never had a moment's thought of giving up."

In 1969 Dora wrote:

"Sometimes people ask me how I came to be working in an Indian village. It is difficult to reply, and I am tempted to say: "By accident". No one asked for me or sent me; I was not a missionary and had no training as a social worker.

"Ten years ago I found myself for the first time able to satisfy a desire that had persisted since my school days – to visit India. The desire had been nourished by the reading of many books, and especially Kipling's *Kim* – a book which I still believe tells more of the real India than scores of travel books and well- documented surveys written since. Geography lessons were to me living experiences, and I felt as if I had touched the soil and rock of India, forded the streams and walked through the bazaars, before I ever set foot in this land. As it happened, I had only one contact in India when the possibility came for me to go, and she was not a village worker, but a writer I had known in Europe, who had settled in Madras. It was this chance which led me to the south rather than to the north of India.

"At first, however, I felt cut off from the real India that

was awaiting me. I was doing a temporary writing job, and was altogether too much in the world of Madrassi servants, who called me 'Madam' and thought how much they could get out of me. Then I was introduced to some people who went weekly to distribute medicines in a village. Walking there, on parched sandy soil, between low-eaved huts of palm thatch; seeing the women threshing or grinding grain, with their babies hung in cloths swinging from the branches of trees, or bending double in the mud of a paddy field, the water half way up their calves, weeding the young rice; seeing the smoke of cooking fires, seeping through the thatch, and the dust of herds of cows rising in the glow of evening; I said: 'Now I have come'.

"I was asked to live in that village, Mudichur, so as to keep contact with the villagers. Not knowing more than a few words of Tamil – which is the main language of the south – I, with what might seem like foolhardiness, agreed. This village was my trial ground, where I worked out ideas, and learned more than I know how to tell. ...

"Although Indian farming is very different from English farming, the fact that I had dealt with the land myself, with my own hands, and lived in a farming community, made it easy for me to understand the meaning of what I saw, and add new knowledge to the old. I had imagined that coming to India made a complete break in my life. But it was not so; I slowly began to feel that I was on the same road still, and the past began to come back to me with renewed relevance and clarity."

It was at this time that she began her friendship with a young farmer, Seetharama Reddy, who could speak some English, and who took an interest in her work and helped her in many ways.

"He was the first person who showed any real interest in my affairs – not the inquisitiveness or formal enquiries I met with from others. He saw that I was suffering very much from being perpetually on view, and having no chance to cook adequate meals. He started by inviting me to his house during the midday hours, giving me a meal and a place to rest.

"He was about twenty-eight, and lived with his wife, Hamsa, in a small house. They had as yet no children. There was a very small yard, a kitchen, a prayer room, and what he called the hall, which was a slightly larger room partly occupied by tools and baskets. In the yard was a little well; I think it was not more than three feet wide. All the house was of unfaced brick. After eating a well-cooked meal of rice and vegetables, I lay back in an old canvas chair, and tasted peace.

"Seetharama Reddy began to visit the clinic daily. By his advice many people came for treatment who would otherwise have been hesitant about coming. He also helped to fence the dispensary compound which had been left entirely open, with herds of goats passing over it, making it impossible to grow any trees or garden plants. Trees were needed because the clinic building was quite bare and unshaded, and the heat of Madras is fierce in the dry season. Seetharama Reddy came from a high caste and very conservative family. He was censured for helping me, a foreigner, and also because the clinic was open to all without caste distinction."

Seetharama badgered the village council to find a place for Dora and eventually she was offered an old *chattram* which had originally been a place for pilgrims to stay. A memorable scene follows their opening of the long-closed door:

"Thousands of bats flew out. The rooms opened onto a courtyard, and as the interior doors had at some time been removed – probably for firewood – the bats could fly down through the courtyard, and hang up in the rooms, undisturbed, during the daylight hours. Now, for the first time in many years their peace was shattered. We flapped cloths and waved sticks; the rush of bats was so great that we were hit in the face by them, and it is very unusual for a flying bat to hit anything. The floors were many inches deep in bats' dung, and several women spent a whole day carrying this out in baskets. There were many little triangular niches meant for oil lamps. We got the lamps, which are just clay cups with twisted cotton wicks, and lit twenty lights as night came on. We burned incense sticks to take off the smell of the bats' dung and urine. It was only after some days' work that the number of bats really decreased; as long as I lived there, which was for several months, there were always bats. I used to watch them hanging against a whitewashed wall; they might have been supposed to be sleeping, but occasionally they would move. If one moved too near another, the second one would jostle him back, making nasty faces and wrinkling up his little snout.

"The floors were of the dust of ages, which seemed to have no solid bottom, so it was impossible to wash them, or even to sweep them more than superficially. All the walls were crumbling. The four interior rooms were unusable, but two others could be made habitable. After the walls were whitewashed, the courtyard looked charming. I even had some plants in pots. I had a kerosene lamp in my living room, but still kept the little oil lamps glowing round the courtyard. The man in charge of the temple complained that the bats had gone over there."

Dora gives a detailed and sympathetic description of the village, its habits, customs, superstitions and castes, the weather, the land and its cultivation, and festivals. She is particularly fascinated by the caste hierarchy: the village is largely inhabited by Harijans (previously called Untouchables; today the usual term is Dalits) who live in three separate *cheris* (areas), in kutcha houses built of mud and thatch. Dora paints a vivid picture of the life inside and outside of these houses, with red earth decorating their walls and white *kolam* patterns on their thresholds.

The caste village, where the Reddiars, who belong to "a highly respected caste of businessmen and farmers", lived had three streets of pukka houses of brick or stone. In them she saw brilliant arrays of polished brass cooking pots and steel trunks where the best gold-bordered saris were stored. There was a prayer room with images of the gods, and flowers, and incense, for regular worship. The men were generally engaged in cultivation, and used the men and women of the *cheri* as a pool of field labour to be called on when necessary. Dora observed the life of the Reddiar women:

"Because the women of the higher castes do not go out to field work they have a better standard of cooking than the Harijans, who are out all day when there is work to be had, and are often content to boil up some grain in the evening and eat it with a few chillies or turmeric sauce. However, the Reddy women, even if they do not work in

84

the fields, are usually hard workers in their way; like their husbands they are very alive to prices and values, they know the measure and the worth of everything; they can choose good grain from inferior, deal with tradesmen and all the kinds of hawkers of pots, pans, saris, and domestic requirements who come round the village; they can strike a hard bargain, and so earn the respect of the sellers. (I had early learnt that you are not expected to give the price asked. If you do, you are thought to be a fool, and not respected. Bargaining, which is full of wit, pleasantries and even what sounds like abuse, but taken in good part, is not only one of the pleasures of life, but a way of arriving at a deal satisfactory to both parties.) These women do all the sifting and grinding necessary for Indian cooking, where all products come in their natural state, and need preparation. They attend to the storage of grain, and dry and preserve various fruits and vegetables."

The castes living nearby also included a community of traditional rat and snake catchers, whose skills were much valued by the farmers; a potter's family who welcomed Dora to watch them at work; a blacksmith and a carpenter. There were also Christians, and there was a Christian school set up by the Church of South India for the Christian Harijans (many Harijans had converted to Christianity).

Dora reflects at length about caste:

"In my days in the Communist Party, if we had occasion to consider India, it was said that industrialisation would cause the breakdown of caste, when all worked together at the same machine or bench. I found that it was by no means as simple as this. The easy assumption shows no understanding of what constitutes caste behaviour. Some

85

of the young men of the Reddy families had obtained jobs at the factories on the Grand Trunk Road. One, in particular, a friend of Seetharama Reddy and a frequent visitor at our dispensary in quiet hours, was working at Standard Motors. He cycled the three miles to work carrying his mid-day meal in one of the stainless steel 'tiffin carriers' which are in common use; he would not eat in the canteen. After work he bathed and changed into a clean dhoti before he took his evening meal. He would be perfectly friendly with the Harijan who worked next to him, but he would not share his food, or marry into his family. When this man did marry, it was strictly within caste, to a bride chosen by his parents. I attended his wedding, which was celebrated with the fullest orthodox Hindu rites, performed by a Brahmin. I have found that this is quite typical."

Even Seetharama, after he had visited Dora in her clinic, would have to bathe and put on fresh clothes. His wife, Hamsa, was uneasy about his mixing with the patients and once, when a large scorpion was found in the house, she regarded it as a sign that he had become somehow polluted.

Daily life in the village challenged many of Dora's assumptions:

"But the strangest thing to me was to live in a caste society. It was not as I had imagined it. As a communist I had always been completely egalitarian. I knew that Gandhi had championed the Untouchables, and deplored the disabilities under which they suffered. Now, in independent India, under the new constitution, all were equal before the law; the word 'untouchable' was not used; all had the right to enter temples; Harijans had wells dug for them, housing colonies set up, and special privileges in education, including scholarships based not on academic performance but on the simple fact of belonging to a 'backward' community, caste or tribe. I found that all high-school children had their caste origin fully stated in their school record books and they were anxious to be recorded as belonging to as 'backward caste' because this meant the possibility of one of these scholarships, with free hostel food and books provided. I had thought that there would be resentment among the lower castes and non-caste people, against the higher ones, and there would be many ways in which they could be helped to better their lot. On the contrary, there was much resentment among Brahmins because they had no scholarships or other privileges, such as reserved places in high schools and colleges; they called themselves the 'new depressed class', and countered by getting control of the administrative jobs in many factories, appointing their caste brothers and relatives, so that many businesses were run entirely by Brahmins.

"I could see that caste was remarkably tenacious, but did not know what fed its inner life. Caste permeates every detail of living, dress, behaviour, profession, religious observance, style of cooking, even the use of certain spices and condiments. It is far more than a set of rules which can be written down. It forms a total picture of how it is proper to behave. Indians are very sensitive to the small details which make up this picture, and can place a person with at least a fair degree of accuracy from just a brief meeting or an encounter on a bus. It is like an instinct, and they do not make mistakes."

Dora tried to find some guidance in Gandhi's thoughts about the issue, particularly admiring his tireless work to uplift the Harijans:

"Gandhi began by upholding caste rules, especially where they concerned marriage and food. Later, he came to the conclusion that caste was originally good, but had been distorted, and encrusted with abuses. He would not defend any caste rule which caused suffering; his deep sympathy with the outcastes forbade that. Towards the end of his life he could be quoted as saying that caste must be abolished. But always in his mind there was an ideal, like the sun shining through clouds, of a society based on duty and service, not on competition."

Turning to the *Baghavad Gita*, Dora found and pondered the concept of *dharma*, often translated as 'duty' but more subtle and meaningful than that: dharma "may more rightly be compared to a path which must be trod." The importance to Indians of following one's own dharma, however imperfectly, was well understood by Dora and she had to explain this, many times, to western volunteers who complained about arranged marriages and other aspects of family life that they found unacceptable.

Throughout these years Alison is keen to get some of Dora's writing about India into print and Dora begins sending numerous articles and pictures, although the quality of the photos is never good enough. Some stories are published in *Blackwood's* magazine and some in newspapers, but there are many rejections too. Even in these early days Dora is thinking of writing a memoir and keen also to describe ordinary Indian village life. By 1969 she writes, "I got a book about three-quarters written, quite some time ago. It was factual but it was in the form of letters from a woman who had gone to live in an Indian village, to a man in England (or to a woman in England, it really doesn't matter) ... I think I can finish it now, and let it sink or swim ..." It appears no copy of this exists. In 1972 we read in a letter to Alison,

> "I am now really getting down to writing a book. It developed into practically an autobiography because I find it impossible to explain what I thought about India without explaining about Hungary, and impossible to explain Hungary without writing about the Communist Party, and impossible to explain why I joined the CP without describing my childhood ... like a series of doors opening backwards. Without this, it's just another of a kind of book of which I think there are too many, descriptions of undertakings of various kinds in remote parts of the world, without any exploration of basic motives."

When Dora arrived in Mudichur in 1960 there were no buses on the roads and no doctor within reach except by bullock cart. In 1962, a bus route had been opened to Madras and a free Government clinic had been started in the nearest small town, Tambaram. She knew it was time to seek fresh challenges, later reflecting:

> "I had started my adult life looking to Distributism for a society in which commercial gain would not be the dominant motive. I had turned to Communism because I thought it would weld humanity into a social order in which service to the community would be to the benefit of all. I had not found what I looked for. But now I saw, in this unremarkable and unknown village, that one slender thread of thinking ran through it all."

Chapter 7

CREATING SEVA NILAYAM:
'HOME OF SERVICE'

Go, and do what comes.

I t was a bulldozer driver who happened to be working near
Mudichur who suggested the idea of moving to his uncle's
village near Madurai, close to the southern tip of India.

> "Here Seetharama and I were given a small room in a
> village house, and we were joined by his wife, Hamsa.
> Then we were given a chance to build a small thatched
> hut of two rooms in a very tiny garden."

Dora's adventurous spirit must have been tested to the limits at
this time: she told me once that their first lodgings were in "a
yard full of dirty boys and goats". There would have been no
running water and no sanitation except the nearby field. One
can imagine her determinedly meeting and even relishing the
challenge; she was undoubtedly captivated by the landscape.

> "Grey rocks rise above the green valleys and the good red
> earth of the cultivated land. To the north the Kodai hills
> stand like a wall, often cloud-capped, with the highest
> point in Perumalmalai at 9,000 feet. The ascent is by a
> winding mountain road passing through plantations of
> coffee, oranges, bananas, jack fruit and eucalyptus. The
> mountains often seem to melt into mist and rain or open
> up into glorious sunsets where earth and sky seem as one.

"A great valley, thirty miles wide, and 1,000 feet above sea level, runs between two spurs of the Western Ghats. On the north the mountain wall rises 7,000 feet, with deep forests in its clefts, and white clouds creeping along well below the summit. On the south is a tumbled area of rocky hills, impassable except for goat tracks.

"The valley is thickly populated, and, except for some barren stretches, it bears crops of rice, maize, onions, cotton and chillies. The soil is red, and the villages are for the most part built of red mud. In the larger villages are some two-storeyed houses of brick and stone, built by rich men, and much painted and decorated, but most of the dwellings are thatched huts in narrow lanes, which are always muddy because the waste water of the houses seeps into them. Many 'houses' actually consist of yards in which cattle and goats are kept at night, and people sleep; a few small rooms opening off serve mainly as store rooms, or for use in cases of sickness or the birth of babies. Often a number of families share a yard. This crowded way of life is typical of hill regions, where there has always been danger from wild animals.

"Our district is inhabited mainly by the Thevar caste, which is scheduled as a 'criminal caste' by the Indian government, because robbery was their hereditary occupation. I have heard that they originated from the army of one of the South Indian kings, which was disbanded, and left without any resource but robbing. The country, with its towering rocks and hidden valleys, was very suitable for this profession. Under the British government some of the most notorious villages had to submit to the finger-printing of all their inhabitants, and the police visited them at night to count the people and see that they were all inside. Little by little the Thevars have become settled farmers, but old customs die hard, and there are still some villages known for robberies.

"There are a few other castes besides the Thevars, mainly Chettiars and Gownders, who are the larger landowners, and used in the past to be frequent victims of the Thevars. The Thevars themselves are happy-go-lucky people, noisy, talkative, quarrelsome, sympathetic and friendly. Their women work in the fields, which is in one way an advantage, because if a woman is deserted or left a widow, she can be independent. In fact, Thevar women can divorce their husbands, and widows sometimes marry again, or at least keep house for another man."

Much as Dora admired the liveliness and strong character of the Thevars, with many neighbouring families belonging to that caste, staff and volunteers at Seva Nilayam had to deal pragmatically with their fearsome reputation for criminality. Staff had to take turns to sleep on top of building materials for fear of losing them, and as there had been cases of cattle stealing in the area, a staff member was obliged to sleep in front of the cowshed. Mr. Reddy used to characterise the Thevars in these terms: "They say, if you give me a chance to steal from you, you are a fool; and if I don't take that chance, I'm the fool." (These words came back to me when I lived in a Thevar village in the remote Varusanadu valley and was forever finding household items gone after people had been to visit. One day a doll went missing; on a routine call to a patient's house a few weeks later we spotted it in a glass-fronted cupboard surrounded by flowers and incense. It was being worshipped like a statue of Krishna. We had no hesitation in stealing it back.)

Within a short time, delighted and fascinated with the area and its people, Dora and Reddy set to work.

"We bought a small plot of land, just over three and a half acres, dug a well, and put up our first buildings. Seetharama Reddy's help was necessary for this purchase because, as a foreigner, I could not own land in India, and only after Seva Nilayam became a Registered Society could it be purchased in that name. Seetharama Reddy bought it in his own name and later transferred it at cost to Seva Nilayam.

"A Swedish lady missionary who helped with the business of registration said, 'You must choose a name. Something like Seva Nilayam, which means Home of Service'. I said, 'Let it be Seva Nilayam', and, so without any argument or discussion, the name was fixed. Slowly we built up our institution, without any showy plans or lofty calculations. We choose the symbol of a tree because it grows quietly and steadily, increasing in strength and following its own nature. Our buildings were made with mud walls and red tiled roofs, the style of village houses. Our first building, which now contains the kitchen for our working staff and any visitors who come, has walls three feet thick and an arched verandah opening on the garden where blue morning glory and red and yellow bougainvillea are always in flower. Some of the other early mud buildings have been replaced by brick but without any alteration in style. We have never employed a contractor, but Seetharama Reddy took responsibility, working himself with local masons."

Dora writes to her brother, Frank Scarlett: "I feel very much in the stream of life. I have not had a dull day since I came to

India. I am getting experience in well digging, coconut planting and the raising of mud walls."

As the work progressed and her knowledge and understanding of local life deepened, a philosophy of working on a human scale emerged:

"There are two ways of working in India. One is to make a plan, collect money to carry it out, and set up a hospital, a sanatorium, an agricultural project, or a centre for research. I would never say that these are not crying needs, and there is certainly much to be done in almost every field one can think of. But the other way is simply to go, and do what comes. And in this way people will accept you as one of themselves, and you can know things, and do things for them, which would otherwise be impossible. You don't make mistakes, because your plans are never more than one step in advance of your practice; you spend money only as you get it, and as you don't build high you can't fall far.

"We are a small family, and we don't want to grow into a big institution, and lose our fun and comradeship in the process. We are under no illusion that we can help the whole of India. We must leave that to the big organisations; but here we are at home."

As part of that small family, volunteers were crucial to the early days of Seva Nilayam clinic and farm. They came from many countries, the USA, Australia and New Zealand, the UK, France and Scandinavia. Some had Quaker connections. Sometimes they brought useful skills, especially those with medical training; others found they could turn their hand to new tasks. Dora wrote with her usual wry humour of one American volunteer who was an expert on antique silver spoons:

> "It would be difficult to imagine anything further removed from the wild countryside in which he worked, cheerfully carrying sand to fill the pits we dug for coconut trees."

Dora pays many tributes to their contributions, but is under no illusions as to where Western volunteers can go wrong. She recalls in a letter to Alison,

> "[M]ost of us go through a period in which we think our ideas are just what the world needs, and perhaps take some kind of pledge that we will devote our lives to remaking the world. When I was growing up, I had no means whatever of making any impact on anyone except a few school friends of the same age. Later, when I joined the Communist Party, I found that, although it did give one a feeling of power, that power could never be individual. The party was a vast organisation in which I was an inconsiderable cog. But now the system of sending out volunteers gives the idealistic young an undreamed amount of power and freedom. They come right into contact with the people they want to alter, and as long as their activities are on the whole in accordance with the ideas of the organisation that sends them out, they can innovate and experiment as they wish. What saves the situation is the age-old conservatism of India. The volunteers (bless their simple hearts) think that the Indians will accept with gratitude what they are told because this wisdom comes from a more 'advanced' section of the world."

She is at pains to point out that the individualism of the west is not without its problems, and the traditions of India must be understood, and cannot be dismissed out of hand. For example, volunteers would often criticise the custom of arranged marriages.

> "They always underestimate the extent religion is entwined with family life, and the reality of the conceptions of *dharma* (one's duty in life) and *karma* (one's destiny which is determined according to strict justice). They also fail to get hold of the idea of privilege which is so real to Indians – it is a great privilege, right, and duty, for a mother to choose a son's bride, and an act of virtue and piety if she chooses well. The girl or boy wants a mate so chosen, because in accepting such a marriage they are fulfilling their dharma, meriting the blessing of their parents and the gods, and laying a secure foundation for their future. Somehow this doesn't seem real to volunteers, who go around India sleeping with their girlfriends, but it's this blindness that makes them commit mistakes. ... Volunteers are very eager to pick on any example of hardship or rebellion – a girl who is married to an old widower, or a young man who wants to travel and see the world before marriage – but they don't see that an arranged marriage, which is a family affair, makes Indians feel part of the great stream of life, in a way which the gratification of individual desire can never do. I'm not saying what's right or what's wrong, but the first thing is to understand."

Dora was very sensitive to perceived differences in living standards, and this reinforced Seva Nilayam's commitment to live as simply and frugally as possible. Volunteers were expected to live according to these principles and be content with a very small stipend, spartan rooms and such food as was available.

"[Westerners] don't understand what a terrific impact their wealth makes in a poor country. They want to buy presents for people who never had a luxury, or children who never had a toy except sticks and stones, leaves and berries. They can't understand what you do to people's minds by displaying wealth before them."

By knowing "too little of the complex and powerful web of Indian domestic and religious life" they tend to see each idea or custom as something separate:

"[O]ne is beautiful, one is deplorable, one is incomprehensible, one is disgusting. They often sincerely love India, and study Indian music or art; they collect statues of gods, learn Indian cooking recipes, wear saris and visit temples. But I haven't met one who has any understanding of the invisible but extremely tough web that binds all these things together in Indian life. You can't pick out the bits you like."

The volunteers formed an essential part of the Seva Nilayam team, working alongside the staff recruited locally. For Dora it was important not to have too many Westerners at any time. Tony Huckle, a volunteer in 1974-5, recalls:

"Dora was somewhat ambivalent about volunteers. For 20 years Seva Nilayam was highly dependent on expatriate nurses but Dora was also at times uncomfortable with volunteers' failure to appreciate some of the subtleties of Indian village culture and at times inappropriate behaviour, especially if sex and relationships were involved. At times, if there were a number of young westerners in residence, they tended to dominate the kitchen conversation and overwhelm the "Indian-ness"

Dora was trying to achieve.

"Dora was always *periyamma* [respected older aunt] and that title was symbolic of the way SN was run – rather authoritarian by western standards but not so unusual in India. The staff at Seva Nilayam were somewhat in awe of her, keeping an obedient distance; and while staff, volunteers and Dora all shared the same food in the same kitchen/dining area there was no escaping the unequal power relationship. Dora always worked hard to do well by the staff, providing presents at Pongal as was the employer's duty – but in a sense this just served to emphasise the paternalism. In conversation, Dora could be kind, interested in others, and enjoy a good discussion but there was always an emotional defensive wall that hardly anyone penetrated."

This natural reserve had been part of Dora's character for many years: in her memoir she portrayed herself as shy and serious. Certainly she was one of those unusual people who talk little about themselves. Although she had one or two friends of her own age in India, she lacked a peer group: she shared Seva Nilayam with much younger western people who had not had the same life experiences as her, and whose light-hearted conversations she must have found at times irritating, if not bewildering, asking in one letter to Alison, "what is a beatnik?" Her ideal of being in India to do good, and serve the poorest, was at odds with the seemingly aimless young westerners who increasingly found their way to India in the 70s. In a letter to Alison she complains:

"India is becoming a playground for people who have decided that they want complete freedom, and will never undertake to do any definite thing for any definite length of time – on principle – and will not let anyone persuade them to shave their beards or wear a shirt."

One of the aimless wanderers who turned up at Seva Nilayam in the mid-70s was John Dalton, from England, who had heard about the clinic on the travellers' grapevine. With no medical skills, he was given gardening work to do, and having proved his commitment through hard graft, graduated to working in the clinic and to becoming a capable, trusted and valued member of staff. Eventually he went for Leprosy Paramedical Worker training and moved out in 1982 to run Arogya Agam, the leprosy hospital just outside Aundipatti. His relationship with Reddy was not easy, for several reasons sketched out by Tony Huckle:

> "One was a certain 'flexibility' in financial matters around the farm and land owned by Seva Nilayam that while pretty much standard practice in rural India would not have passed muster under a stricter moral code. The second, more serious, concerned India's caste system and the discrimination faced by Dalits. There was no overt discrimination at SN, but people knew that Dalits were not as welcome as caste people."

Dora was unwilling to challenge Reddy over this caste issue. She maintained it was not for her to try and change society, but simply to help the poorest: the committed Marxist of the 1940s had learnt from experience. How far the work was compromised by Reddy's treatment of Dalits is hard to estimate. Once Dalton had been trained, he moved to the leprosy hospital, named Arogya Agam (Place of Health), and remained close (as close as anyone could be) to Dora until her death. He still lives and works in India and has led the evolution of Arogya Agam into a centre promoting human rights for the most marginalised (women, Tribals, Dalits, transgender and people living with HIV) and providing medical care for HIV+ patients.

Tony Huckle paints a vivid picture of Dora's daily life in the mid-seventies:

"Dora's day began before dawn with a cup of tea delivered by the cook, who had been up much earlier to light the stove on which the water for the tea was heated. She joined the staff and volunteers for breakfast before the clinic opened at 7am. In my time in the mid-70s she did not work in the clinic but I know she did both earlier and later in SN history. In 1985 she was manning the triage desk. After breakfast Dora might discuss various matters of administration or general things that needed attending to around the place. She spent the mornings writing either letters or her memoir. After lunch she might do a bit of gardening usually with one of the young farm boys assisting her with pruning and watering. She had her bath in the outside bathroom beside her room. There was an evening meal at about 7pm at which people would sit around in the kitchen and chat, and after that she would read in her room. Her room was one of the original mud and tile structures at SN, very basic, with a wooden bed, a desk and a cupboard. The cupboard was locked and contained SN's cash box which at times had quite a lot of money in it. Only Dora, Reddy and the assistant secretary treasurer were allowed to enter the room unaccompanied. She had a box of clothes, a few books and a handful of possessions and a 1920s-era typewriter."

The encounter with another culture, which Dora found so invigorating, demanded much hard work and soul-searching; she was well aware of the "danger that over-enthusiastic volunteers will become disillusioned and embittered. Yet those who do not may advance to a deep understanding of India." Time spent working at Seva Nilayam was for many people a life-changing and profound experience and many were deeply grateful for the unique opportunity Dora had offered them to get so close to South Indian village life and culture.

Returned volunteers founded Village Service Trust, initially to fundraise for the work and support Dora. VST now supports the legacy project Arogya Agam, and also Vasandham, founded in 1987 by Dora's protégé Gunasekaran, which continued and developed the work my husband and I had started in the remote Varusanadu valley. In all her dealings with volunteers, and in her correspondence, Dora insisted on the importance of understanding, respecting and appreciating Indian culture. It was to advance and encourage this all-important knowledge and understanding that Dora began, in 1974, to write *Letters from Seva Nilayam* to well-wishers and friends around the world. It is on these newsletters that the following chapters are based.

Dora at the kitchen door 1969

Chapter 8

"THERE ARE GOOD THINGS HERE":
FOOD AND FARMING AT SEVA NILAYAM

Farming, to us, is not an industry, it is a whole complex of relationships of man with the earth, with animals, and of ourselves with our neighbours.

It was a busy morning in the clinic with long queues waiting to be seen. Often Dora would sit at the table where everyone was greeted and given a number; and she would look carefully at people, often taking their hands, assessing their level of need, sometimes taking them herself to the doctor or into the dressings room. But this particular morning I saw her setting out a stall: "Look," she said to me, "I have made up little plates of fruit from our own garden to sell to the patients as they wait: a piece of papaya, a banana, a piece of jackfruit. I want people to see there are good things here."

The farm and the clinic were intimately connected. Early in the morning the milk was brought in foaming in its brass pail from the cowshed. Eggs were carried in from the hen house, bananas from the garden. On each of my visits, there was always something special: bright green wing beans; new baby carrots, carefully nurtured by Dora; lemon cheese made with their own lemons; home-made yoghurt and ghee. I would often be taken to admire something in the farm or garden: a new-born calf, the brilliant green of the young paddy, the rare flower on the jack fruit tree, a new vine. Precious seeds lay drying on Dora's table, and a nursery of young plants sat outside her room. Working with the land to make it productive, Seva Nilayam shared in the daily labour of most of their neighbours. "He is a very good

103

farmer" was one of Dora's highest forms of praise. Pride in the creation of a productive farm from a featureless patch of ground shines through all the letters on the subject of food and farming.

"Our three and a half acres provides a small farm to produce food for ourselves and the in-patients. At present we are growing groundnuts which are looking very well, and we had this year a very profitable crop of onions. In addition we grow many kinds of vegetables: gourds, beans, carrots, beetroots, radishes, tomatoes and different sorts of greens. We have a very prolific banana patch which bears heavy bunches. We are growing our own rice and getting our own coconuts, and for our milk supply, we have buffaloes and a cow. We also have bullocks for ploughing and pulling the cart. We sell our surplus produce in the market, but we do not go in for big cash crops. It is a small, compact area of production as dictated by our own needs."[1]

Dora was particularly impressed with the special skills needed by field workers and the tools they used. One newsletter described the ubiquitous digging implement found in most households, the *mun vetti* or, colloquially, *mumti* (literally "soil cutter") which is the main hand tool used in gardening. She celebrates the perfect timing by which the water is made to run along successive irrigation channels into the small patches of ground ready for cultivation. The land at Seva Nilayam was not only productive, but beautiful:

"The flower garden is my concern and this is not just a pastime. I think that every place should be made beautiful. There are many spots where one can sit, relax, and talk to visitors, and we

---

[1] *A Short History of Seva Nilayam 1988*

get ample testimony that these things are appreciated. There is the glorious Gul Mohur or flame tree, entirely covered with scarlet blossoms in May; the Indian laburnum, with drooping gold chains; the frangipani, or temple tree, which strews the ground with waxy-white, fragrant, gold-centred blossoms and the bougainvillea with rose, red or purple flowers. In every odd corner we have planted hibiscus in shades of yellow, orange and red, and for contrast, the brilliant blue Morning Glory ramps over the roof."[2]

The ubiquitous goats, however, had to be kept out with thorny fences, as "an interest in goats and in gardens can scarcely co-exist."

For agriculture to flourish there must be water. Seva Nilayam experienced droughts and floods on a regular basis, the failure of the monsoon meaning families and even whole villages were forced to relocate in times of water shortage. The need for reliable supplies of water was a constant concern, and the lowering of the water table caused by the deepening of wells, this in turn facilitated by increasing availability of electricity for pump-sets, was noticed with much anxiety. The joy at the coming of the rains was deeply felt.

> "In India the question is not: 'Did you have fine weather?' but 'Have you had good rain?' Rain is happiness; people go barefoot in the mud, laughing and smiling. If it rains when a visitor comes, they say: 'You are a luck-bringer – rain has followed you'."

Feeding the in-patients good food was as important a part of

---

[2] *Gardening 1978*

their treatment as the medicines and Dora delighted in the simple kitchen and the meals produced there, often reminding me with a smile: "All H.G!" (I think this was a war-time slogan denoting home-grown food.)

Dora celebrates the growth and development of the farm:

"Two weeks ago our fields, flooded ready for rice planting, were like smooth mirrors reflecting the passing clouds and the dark- leaved coconut trees around their edges. Then the women came, and pressed the thin, grass-like seedlings into the mud, one by one. Now these fields are an expanse of brilliant green, with the shining water visible only between the stems. The season promises well.

"Twelve years ago this land was totally unproductive, without a well or a tree, or a single useful plant. We were living in a village two miles distant, and had to walk to the land to do some preliminary work, marking boundaries and choosing a site for the well and the house. The whole area was so featureless that I had to use a tall termites' nest as a landmark by which to know when I reached it.

"The well was the first necessity, not only so that we could irrigate the land, but so that we could make bricks and mix cement for the building. Wells in this part of the country are usually fourteen feet square, and at least thirty feet deep, to give sufficient storage capacity.

"While the local well-diggers were at work, with spades and crowbars, hammers and chisels, we prepared to plant coconut trees in a ring round the area, as it was time to do this. Our volunteer worker, John Davis, [the antique spoons man] walked here every day – there were no buses on the road then, and we had no vehicle – and made ready the pits for tree planting, putting in earth and sand in the right proportions. It was heavy work, and until the well-diggers struck a spring, he had to carry his flask of drinking water. There was no shop anywhere near at which he could buy anything. We have never forgotten this pioneering work, and I often think of it when I see the coconut trees, now thirty feet tall, standing like guardians and bearing their gift of nuts.

"In our yard are cows, buffaloes, and working bullocks, and their manure keeps up the fertility of the soil. In our tree plantation, which also serves as a windbreak against the fierce wind in the time of the south-west monsoon, are mangoes, guavas, papayas and kapok. We give employment to local people, five or six steadily, and many more for planting, weeding and harvesting. In 1968 and the years following, we bought some further plots of land, to set up a leprosy clinic, and we farm these in the same way. We now have a total of 15 acres. Rice is the one crop which South Indians wish above all to grow, but besides that we grow maize and other grains, groundnuts, chillies, tomatoes, brinjals (egg-plants), onions, sweet potatoes, and a variety of vegetables. We have laying hens to provide for our own needs, not for market.

"Our farm is of a special kind; it is a setting and support for our medical work. It provides rehabilitation work for our leprosy patients; only too often those who are stricken with this disease believe that they are unemployable, so responsibility for irrigation, or feeding cattle, or tending a vegetable plot helps to give them back self-respect. Our other in-patients, too, help in any way they can. They shell groundnuts, pack tomatoes in baskets, drive off crows, carry straw, feed the calves. All of this involves a very active and social life. We would not, even for a larger financial return, plant a cash crop over the whole area. We would not use a tractor, which could be driven by one man, leaving the local villagers without work. I do not deny that tractors have their uses, especially where new areas of untilled land are brought into cultivation, but for us it would have no meaning, and only impair our relationships with the local people.

"Farming, to us, is not an industry, it is a whole complex of relationships of man with the earth, with animals, and of ourselves with our neighbours. At planting and harvest time a group of polished brass and aluminium 'tiffin carriers' will be ranged under a tree; these contain the mid-day meals of the casual workers. Babies are slung in hammocks from the trees, and a family goat may be brought along for a bit of extra feed. When we have had rain and the grass is lush, one of our in- patients may be seen leading a cow along the field borders to graze. A boy who was a tubercular patient, now completely cured, drives our buffaloes out to wallow in a nearby water tank. His mother, who is a widow, sweeps our paths, does weeding, and all kinds of odd jobs. When work is urgent, as when a harvest must be brought in before rain comes, our clinic staff, when the day's patients have been treated, are off into the fields too.

"We have not branched out into any new and spectacular methods which might upset the structure of local farming. We farm as our neighbours do, but we try to do it extremely well, to the best of our ability. We help and advise them, and often get help in return.

"We use many of the new and improved varieties of seeds,

but we are quite aware that these have disadvantages as well as advantages, and are not going to solve all the farmer's problems. We are willing to try out new ideas, and think up some for ourselves, but we will not depart from our mixed and 'family' farming. We are aware that it might seem trifling and laborious to those who are after big money or want to make big changes. But we have come through some bad seasons of drought without shortage. We are able to sell our surplus to those who need it, and obtain from them what we need. Market prices may fluctuate wildly, and of course, we are always glad if we get a good return for what we sell, but in all these years we have never been in want. We have many good things. In our garden we can always pick some fruit, some herbs or spices; we have coconuts to use in our cooking, vegetables and fresh eggs. Above all, we have made friendships which no money can buy."[3]

Dora had very lean times in the early days and lamented to Alison Selford that she had strapping young male volunteers to feed and very little available:

"For many weeks it has been impossible to get wheat or any kind of flour. For several weeks we couldn't get sugar. Meat – insipid goat, with bits of lights and unmentionables in it which we should call 'pieces for the dog' in England – is 2/6 a pound.

... For a long time, people haven't been able to get rice without spending hours in a queue, and two women were crushed to death ... I have two large volunteers to feed, one American and one Dane over 6 feet high and hungry in proportion. The mere effort of amassing enough food every day is enough to wear one out. Small soapy potatoes

3 *Farming 1974*

are 1/- a pound."

Alison offers to send food parcels, and much of the rest of the correspondence over two decades is about what to send and how to send it, with Alison often getting it wrong. Dora preferred everything to be sewn Indian-style into cloth parcels. She is at first grateful for the flour, and sugar, and makes cakes; tinned cheese is much enjoyed, and any dried fruit and soups. At the end of the 60s Alison writes, "Today I sent off 6lb of flour, 4lb of sugar, 1lb of sultanas, 6 ½ oz grated cheese, three tins of minced beef, two tins of kippers, two tins of herring roe, some packets of powdered soup, and my novel, *No Need of the Sun*. I also put in a little chocolate."

The next parcel contains a similar set of items and a few old copies of the *Morning Star*. Dora replies that flour and sugar are now obtainable (on the black market), and, horrified by the cost of postage, begs Alison to stop sending such heavy items. Dried fruits are much prized and hoarded to put in fruit cakes, but glacé cherries sent in small plastic tubs invariably break or are broken into by the customs officials and leak everywhere. Eventually, and perhaps a little exasperated, Dora sends a list of what she would like:

"Best tea (all the best is exported)
China tea
A tin of Camembert or other real cheese (not processed)
A tin of good shortbread
Grated Parmesan cheese
Raisins and sultanas
A jar of Chinese ginger in syrup
Crystallised ginger and crystallised (real) fruit
Chocolate (it doesn't travel well, gets squashed and
sticky, but Toblerone is very hard and well packed)
Pure cocoa"

It is interesting that as the years go by, and Dora becomes more habituated to the Indian diet, she asks less and less for western items like these. She did always enjoy home baked bread, with baking soda if yeast was not available, but the 'biscuit tin' oven was not often used.

"Most people know that the mainstay of this part of the country is rice. While it is growing, or still in the husk, it is called paddy and only when milled does it become rice: *arisi*. To grow paddy a lot of water is required: it stands in water until the latest stage when it is dried off before harvesting. The fields around us, which were a brilliant green a month ago, are now turning golden, and some have been harvested, and only dry stubble remains.

"Paddy is not the only grain grown here, there is a small maize, rather like a millet, called *cholam* and this is, in fact, the staple diet of many of the poorer people, who cannot grow rice, or afford to buy it every day. There are *ragi*, *tennai* and *cumbu*, all tasty and nutritious grains, which can be grown with less water, but these are light crops: only paddy is a heavy producer.

"South Indians are often blamed for conservatism in diet. A friend visiting here asked me 'If water is scarce, why do they not grow something else, that takes less water?' I asked him what he would suggest and he said, 'Wheat'. But wheat, which is grown in North India, belongs to the temperate zone. These plants are distributed across the world in the zones in which they originated from wild grains. People love them because they have been the food of life from time immemorial. Such plants take on a sacred character. Just as wheat, and the bread made from it, have had a religious connotation in Europe, so rice is

111

enshrined in the rites of South Indians. It is offered in temples, and at marriages; it is dedicated to the goddess of plenty and is a symbol of fertility. Every farmer who can possibly grow even a small patch of paddy wants to do so: he feels then he is a proper farmer. Not far from Seva Nilayam there is an area of very barren land. The rock is near the surface and the fields are littered with stones. Here people can only cultivate a little grain during the monsoon, and they can only grow *cholam*. In the hot weather the area is like a desert. Such cultivators, of course, cannot live on their own produce; they also work as labourers for others, or even at some quite different jobs. The ideal farmer should have his paddy fields and plantations of coconuts and bananas, all lush and heavy yielding crops, and all essentials for good living.

"Many people in the West believe that all Indians are starving. This is largely the result of the fact that bad news is news, and good news is not. The Indian climate is violent and uncertain. Every year there will be a drought somewhere, and a flood somewhere perhaps at the same time. But the country is vast, and the millions of people who carry on from day to day with what seems to them normal and sufficient food find no place in the news. Every morning I can see parties of field workers, many of them boys and women, going out at first light, some with brass vessels on their heads, finely polished and glinting in the early sun. Ask them to open them and you will see a mass of pinkish grey boiled maize, and a small cup of vegetables, turmeric or chillies. But they can do a hard day's work on this food. They are lean and tough, and I have never found any foreigner, used to a high protein diet, who can keep up with them.

"Are there then no needs for better diet? Yes, there are. We find undernourished people, especially children, in our clinic every day. This may be due to many causes, but seldom to sheer lack of food. As milk is not abundant in tropical countries it is difficult to find a good invalid diet. People who have been ill, and have no appetite for the normal food are unable to afford the milk, eggs, or protein foods which would set them up. Children at weaning often go through a dangerous period, if they go straight from the breast to the rather harsh *cholam*. If they fall sick it is often very hard to get them through convalescence, and they can develop chronic diarrhoea, eye defects and even blindness, through lack of vitamins. But there are hosts of jolly, healthy children in the villages who have never had these misfortunes. There are old people left with no one to support them, and if they cannot beg they may be actually short of food. For these reasons we give in our clinic, to selected cases, milk powder, some very good blends of maize and soya flour which come through relief organisations, and *Winfood*, a flour made of sprouted grain which we buy from a Gandhian institute in the area.

"There is also an idea abroad that village people are unhappy because they think they are poor, and long for more luxuries. In our view, based on years of experience, they are, if anything, too contented. A day of work, and a huge plate of some boiled grain at night fills them with satisfaction. They eat in bulk, far more than I, or any of my co-workers could ever eat, but they tend to neglect the supply of vegetables, and some more varied foods, which would guard against deficiency diseases. They think it great good fortune to have rice and mutton on festival days. This is why we have a productive vegetable garden ourselves, and try to encourage the use of tomatoes, greens, and the local vegetables. But we do not underestimate the difficulties of families which have no land of their own, and in which all the members may be out working and return only at night to cook a meal.

"We have one great advantage over city people. We live among growing food, we see it every day in all stages, we harvest it ourselves, and we know what we are getting. It is not processed, packaged or chemically treated, and even in poverty we have pure food."[4]

Central to the life of Seva Nilayam as a community was the kitchen. Meals for resident volunteers and staff were taken in the long shady room, with non-resident staff bringing their tiffin boxes and sitting in the enclosed verandah. Stainless steel plates and cups were used, and people generally followed the local custom of eating with the right hand.

"The kitchen is the heart of the house. When we came to this place, which was an empty field, the first necessity was to dig a well and arrange for a water supply. (At that stage water had to be carried in earthen pots, and only after a few years could we arrive at the luxury of pipes and taps. Almost all the water supply of rural India and even much of the town supply is still carried in such pots).

"When putting up the first building we could not afford factory made bricks. We used the clay which could be dug out on the spot and we employed village labourers to raise the walls. These walls are three feet thick and they carry a red-tiled roof. Such houses, like the adobe buildings of

---

[4] *Food 1977*

Central and South America will last indefinitely if the roof is kept in good repair.

"This kitchen is 29 feet long and it has an extension on the east side, which was made later, by covering in a verandah with light metal mesh, and digging out two arches to lead to it. This annexe looks on to the garden, which is a mass of colour, with red bougainvillea, blue morning glory and golden leaved crotons. The kitchen wall on the west side has only small windows, because of the fierce wind which blows from June to September bringing frequent dust storms.

"There are two stoves in the kitchen. One is the type designed for the Indian Government, under the name *Smokeless Chula*. It is an advance on the typical village kitchen stove, from which the smoke has to escape through a small aperture, or just seep through the thatch. The smokeless chula, when well-made, has a good draught, and a chimney rising above the roof tiles. This stove has a top tiled with squares of black *cuddapah* stone, a very durable material which can be easily cleaned, and which provides a heated area on which pots can be kept warm. We burn some wood, but chiefly shells and stems from our coconut trees, which are rich in oil, and make a good blaze. The milk is best boiled on a wood stove as it can be kept simmering for a long time, resulting in a thick layer of cream. The other stove burns gas, which is produced by our Gobar Gas plant in the garden behind the kitchen. Such gas plants are being popularized by the authorities in an attempt to lessen the wood cutting which is denuding many hill slopes, and defeating the Government's efforts at re-afforestation. The gas plant is fed by fresh cow dung mixed with water, and produces colourless and odourless methane gas, which rises in a metal drum and is piped to two gas burners inside the kitchen. The manure which has been through the gas plant retains its full value as a fertiliser.

"You take off your shoes before entering the kitchen, as this is the custom in South India. Even the most squalid village huts enjoy this mark of respect. The kitchen floor is painted red and is very pleasant and cool to the feet. There is a blue painted cupboard and storage tins also painted blue. The walls are white-washed, and this is done once a year, in preparation for the feast of Pongal in January. There are no chairs, but a number of wooden benches made by a local carpenter. Water comes through two taps supplied from a raised tank into which it has been pumped from our well. Over the years this kitchen has received many visitors. It has seen the unremitting daily work of the household, and varied styles of cooking, all based on the local products of the earth. It has been the scene of debates and (I must not deny) some quarrels and differences of opinion, but also the bringing of news from afar, the making and strengthening of friendships, and the enjoyment of good food. It is the heart of the house and of Seva Nilayam itself."[5]

Dora was proud of what they had achieved on their small patch of land. From nothing, they had created a beautiful and productive place, where farm and the clinic were inseparable, each enhancing the work of the other. At a time when the "green revolution" was in full force and farmers were being persuaded to use new varieties of seeds produced by big corporations and to buy large farm machinery to replace manual labour, she held

---

5 *The Kitchen 1985*

fast to traditional methods of small family farming.

As might be expected, India has taken the opposite track: the number of tractors now in use in the rural areas is both a cause and an effect of the numbers of people migrating to the cities for work. Farmer suicides due to unsustainable debt, drought and crop failure have been widely reported in recent decades. Dora's writings on food and farming, as on so many other topics, document a way of life that, despite its hardships, had the beauty, diversity, integrity and, above all, the authenticity she sought.

Chapter 9

+—————•—————+

A HOLISTIC APPROACH TO HEALTH CARE

We would like to be the Family Doctor to this particular patch of rural India.

The Seva Nilayam approach to medical care considered the patient as a person in context, not a "case". Over and over again the emphasis was on the relationship between the healer and the sick person:

> "Every day, and in every hour of the clinic work, we can see that even the best medicines will not have their value unless we know much about the patient, and can establish a relationship. Such a relationship is achieved by speaking, but also, in a very important way, by looking."

Dora would quote an old doctor she had known: "For one mistake made by not knowing, ten mistakes are made by not seeing," and she would often take patients' hands and hold them as they spoke to her, feeling as well as listening and looking, so as to fully understand the person's situation and the reason for their ill-health. Dom Helder Camara's insight: "When I give the poor bread, they call me a saint; when I ask why they are hungry, they call me a Communist" is reflected in Dora's observation, "All medical questions are social questions."

> "The hands always tell their story. There is a widespread belief that illness can be diagnosed by looking at the hands, and patients will very often spread out their hands without being asked. ... Looking at them we see days of toil, of grasping tools, hauling on ropes, binding sheaves,

118

pulling weeds, cutting firewood."

The treatments were simple, some might now think primitive, and frugality – "we would be ashamed to waste even a Rupee when there are those in want" – was a priority; but where it was necessary, there was an open-hearted willingness to spend money, if it was the only way someone could be offered a chance of life.

"Belief in the value of the individual is our justification for trying to help all those in need. We cannot save the world; we can help only those who come to us ... But if we can save one person from death or lifelong disability; if we can cure a child of leprosy in the early stages; or if we can restore a sick baby to health, for that patient, or that parent, the whole world is altered."

The complexities of offering health care in a society in transition from the traditional to the modern are understood through long and profound experience:

"'Medicine' does not mean just one system of knowledge and practice, of measurable drugs given in prescribed doses. In any ancient civilisation, or strong tribal culture, it is deeply entwined with the social and traditional life of the people. Newcomers to India from the West tend to regard their own allopathic [i.e. western] system as the norm, and so they sometimes find the behaviour of the people foolish or inexplicable. ... Allopathic medicine has conquered many diseases once thought to be incurable. But at the same time it has done violence to the old, entwined systems of belief and practice in which people have lived so long. It has slighted and disregarded people's confidence in the powers of nature and the ability of the body to cure itself.

"And so, at Seva Nilayam, 'We live in the middle of a clash of cultures, and this is deeply interesting, generally frustrating, but often rewarding and enlightening.' Over and over the importance of the relationship between the healer and the patient was stressed, a relationship facilitated by living as closely as possible to the people and understanding their way of life. This kind of work can bring happiness, and 'the kind of happiness I mean is an indication of the rightness of the work'."

But again, she was not unrealistic about the challenges:

"Of course, we are not always radiating smiles. We can get irritated with the patients. Sometimes they start a quarrel among themselves, pushing each other, and arguing in shrill voices. Some are garrulous, and it is hard to sympathise with people who will not stop talking about trifling or imaginary ailments. Some exaggerate their symptoms, and some, for one reason or another, do not tell the truth. Sometimes we feel just too tired to deal with all this. It seems all very far from any idealistic picture of ourselves healing and consoling the afflicted. But then, perhaps, we ask a patient who has come an unusually long distance: 'Why did you come here?' and we get the answer: 'They say you take very good care of people.' So we may feel a bit ashamed of short temper, but also reassured that the deep relationship is there."

The principle of free treatment is discussed at length in the Letter, *Our Choice*. As so often in these letters, there is an unbroken thread winding from Dora's early political education to her life at Seva Nilayam. From today's perspective, her comments on the NHS may appear alarmingly topical.

"All human activity is based on some philosophy, whether this is known to those concerned in it or not. The movements of human society have very deep roots, and their outcome is determined by these roots, as the nature and type of a flower is determined by the underground parts of a plant which are not seen. The theory behind a free health service is that all members of the human family should have the right to health, and all that is needed to preserve and maintain it ... It may be like a dream of a golden age, but in fact it is the only fully human philosophy of medicine."

She had also noticed an increasing incidence of cancer, noting that when they began work in the area there was no cancer ward in the government hospital. She had her own ideas of why cancer was increasing. It had become, and still is, the custom to spray field crops with toxic chemicals, dispensed from a backpack sprayer.

"Usually the farmers admit that they have not read the leaflet enclosed in the bottle of chemical spray. They also admit they never wear any protective clothing. They mix the insecticide by guesswork and without measuring and often far in excess of the recommended proportions. If market conditions are right, they will send the vegetables for sale the day after they have been sprayed, although the directions are, they should wait at least 10 days."

Dora blamed the lack of scientific education, lamenting that farmers "will rush to kill a snake, which might cause death in one person, but they will, without any hesitation, fill the air with poisons which could, many months later, cause the death of a number of people, impossible to count." The toxic chemicals used in agriculture she also blames for the rise in "strange and inexplicable skin troubles" on the legs of farm workers who walk through treated crops. As always, Dora's mission is to understand and to treat the patient as a whole person, knowing his work, his home circumstances and his difficulties.

One thing missing from these Letters is any mention of HIV and AIDS, now a major health issue in India, but at the time Dora was active in the clinic the disease was as yet unknown there. Since the eighties an exemplary project to address HIV and AIDS has been set up at Arogya Agam [Place of Health]. This project was originally an outpost of Seva Nilayam undertaking leprosy control work but in 1982 it became a separate institution. During the 1980s the incidence of leprosy fell dramatically with the advent of new drugs that cured the disease in months rather than years. At much the same time the HIV pandemic arrived in India and as increasing numbers of cases were identified locally Arogya Agam began work in this field. Dora was interested in this aspect of the work at Arogya Agam and did welcome subsequent HIV-related work at Seva Nilayam.

The daily work of the clinic is elegantly described in this early letter.

"Seva Nilayam out-patient clinic opens at seven in the morning. Before that, we, the clinic workers, can look out from the kitchen where we are taking our breakfast, and see the first patients waiting.

"This early start is a help to the people. Those who live near, and are not very ill, can have their treatment and go, and need not lose a day's work. Those who have come a long distance the day before, and spent the night nearby, can get away in reasonable time for their homeward journey. Many do this. The climate is kind, and people are hospitable; you can sleep on a verandah or under a tree. We also like to start work while the morning is cool and fresh.

"Lying in bed late is not an Indian vice – if people want some extra sleep, they usually take it in the middle of the day. Even before it was light, we heard parties of field workers going along the road, and the tinkle of goat bells as the flocks were driven up to hill pastures.

"Buses stop at the end of the sandy lane leading to Seva Nilayam, and usually most of the passengers get out there. Others come walking across the fields. They are of all ages – sick babies, young mothers, farmers, workers on tea or coffee plantations, old men and women, Muslims, Hindus, high caste or low caste. All must come in the same way, and wait their turn. As they come to give their names, they see a blue painted tin, and they are asked to put some money in this. It is a collection, and bears no relation to the amount of treatment they receive. Those who cannot afford anything are not refused treatment, nor do they get any less attention. The money obtained from the collection covers only a small part of the monthly medicine bills. Some patients bring presents in kind – perhaps some beans, or garden seeds, a few cardamoms (a much-valued spice) or even grapes or oranges.

"We are here to serve the poor patients, and those who have no medical help. By long experience we are very good at estimating the wealth and social position of patients, and if we think that some of them do not really need our services, we give them a prescription which they can buy for themselves. No one is ever charged for medicine at Seva Nilayam.

"The cases vary from the very slightest – children from the next village with a grazed knee or a stomach ache – to patients with long-neglected wounds which have ulcerated and eaten deep into the flesh, tormenting skin infections, chronic coughs which may be tubercular, or infestation by hookworm, which drains the blood and leaves the patient gasping for breath and near to heart failure.

"We seldom finish the clinic before two or three o'clock. Many patients bring their food – rice in a brass or aluminium pot, or just wrapped in a banana leaf and a cloth. They find a shady spot in which to eat it, and get some water from the pump. The day wears on, and we begin to feel weary; it is with relief that we see the crowd thinning out, and feel a cool breeze when the noontide heat has passed.

"There are many problems. Some patients have to be admitted if we are to have any hope of treating them effectively. They may have spent their last money on the bus, or the last of their strength to reach us. They are sometimes in tears when we cannot admit them. We try to admit as many as really need it, but we are not a hospital, only a clinic with space for fourteen or fifteen in-patients. When they are admitted they receive a mat, a sheet, an aluminium cup and plate, and lie down in a room with a tiled floor and no furniture. They get all food free while they are here; if they had to pay, they would be unable to remain. Also, good food, much of it produced on our own farm, is part of the cure.

"When the last patient has gone, we have to sweep the floor, sterilise the instruments and burn the rubbish. Tomorrow will be another day. Sunday is a holiday, but even then, the in- patients have to be attended to, and we always have to be ready for emergencies. We treat most of the local accidents and cases of sudden, acute illness.

"It is known that we treat the poor, and all patients are equal to us. So none are afraid to come. We are interested in their families, homes, circumstances and occupations, because the more we know about them the more effectively we can treat them. There is an old belief in India that the efficacy of medicine depends on the person who gives it. This is not all superstition; there must be a human relationship between patient and medical worker. People value this, and continue to come, struggling for places on crowded buses or walking over rough roads."[6]

For those who could not be treated at the clinic and dreaded the prospect of being admitted to the big Government Hospital in Madurai, Seva Nilayam found an elegant solution:

"To the patient from a remote village, the hospital is another world. He has not the temerity to say that he cannot wait three days and has not enough money to go home and come back again.

"People in the villages live largely on local produce. They are not used to buying food at city prices. And where can they stay? They are not used to hotels and lodging houses.

---

[6] *The Clinic 1974*

Often they sleep on the sand outside the hospital. Perhaps on a hot night looking up at the stars, and needing no bed cover, this is not worse than their experience at home. But there can be lashing rain or searching wind, the roads may run like rivers and there may not be a dry spot to lie down in. They may meet the morning wet and shivering.

"In this area, busy and crowded, there is a house in a small street. Its name is Anbu Illam. That means the 'Place of Kindness'. Anbu may be translated 'love' but it means respectful affection. A child writing to his mother will begin 'Anbu Amma', 'Dear Mother'. I think in this case kindness is the right word. Any patient who is sent by us, or by another institution, with a letter, and is genuinely waiting for hospital treatment, is given food and a place to sleep free of charge. This means that they can face the prospect of a few days waiting until they are either admitted or sent back to us with their prescription, and they do not wander off looking for shelter.

"I have often written on the theme 'Small is Beautiful' and I think Anbu Illam is a very good example. It was started in response to a felt need. A friend of ours who had spent many years in India found needy patients coming to her door for help. So she took a small room in the same area, where she could meet them, then later she took this house and named it Anbu Illam. She is no longer in India, but Anbu Illam is run by an Indian Committee, and receiving donations to keep its work going.

"It is humble and unpretentious; it is not part of any large scheme. It does not think it is called upon to develop into something else, to be some sort of medical or educational institution. It is content with offering kindness where it is needed."[7]

One of Dora's favourite themes is babies and children. Many of the early letters expound on this topic. The difficulties of obtaining milk powder, and of distributing fairly and carefully a commodity which could be sold for cash, are well set out in a letter noting that milk powder supplies were running short:

"One Friday morning I happened to be coming back to Seva Nilayam on an early bus, having stayed the night with friends in Madurai. The bus looked as if it might have been going to a baby show, it was so crowded with mothers and babies. It would, however, have seemed an unusual show because, although some of the babies were fat and well, others were weak and puny. It was, in fact, carrying them all to our Mother and Baby Clinic, which is held every Friday.

"I knew everybody on the bus, and I was expected to look at all the babies and hear about them. Those on distant seats were held up for me to see. So we had a happy time as the bus bumped along the uneven road between red ploughed fields, past mud-walled villages, and willy-nilly bounced the babies up and down on their mothers' laps. At the stop outside Seva Nilayam the bus was emptied of most of its passengers. We walked down the narrow sandy lane bordered with thorn hedges and turned in at the entrance to our clinic building. The desk was ready, the weight cards in order, and the baby scales set out on the verandah.

"If Friday morning is the busiest, it is also the happiest morning of the week. There are usually about fifty

---

7 *Abu Illam 1981*

mothers present, but instead of only fifty babies there are sixty-five or seventy. How is this? There are fifteen sets of twins. Poor working mothers seldom have enough milk for two babies, and the word has gone round that we are willing to supplement the feed with milk powder, and so twins born within a radius of twenty miles are brought along. We are able to make the birth of twins a joy instead of a misfortune. Almost all twins are called Raman and Lakshmanan, after the heroes of the well-loved Hindu epic the *Ramayana*, if they are boys, and if girls they are called by the equivalent names Ramuthai and Lakshmi. Besides the twins there are a few motherless babies, brought by grandmothers, elder sisters, or sometimes fathers. These depend on us for their life.

"It is not very easy for mothers to get themselves registered in our baby clinic. They have to show real need, and we have to use the milk for those who need it most. We never encourage bottle feeding if breast feeding is possible. We examine the mothers carefully, and those who are sick have to take treatment themselves. If the baby is still young there is a good chance that the mother will get her own milk after some help in the early stages. The most common cause of loss of milk is anaemia due to hookworm, and this is curable. Sometimes the lack of milk is due to sheer hard work and poor food. There is just no surplus nourishment for milk production. Some of the babies have been very ill with dysentery or bronchitis, and need good medical care as well as feeding. The medicines, vitamins, and protein foods we give form quite a heavy item in our expenditure.

"Some of the babies are so tiny and wrinkled when they are first brought that they look hardly human. It is a great joy to see them slowly recovering, putting on weight, getting smooth skins and bright eyes, and laughing back at us when we talk to them.

"We expect mothers to start giving solid food from the age of nine months, so that we can reduce the allowance of milk powder, and give more to those who need it more, the newborn and the very sick. It is a custom in the villages to keep babies at the breast till they are well over a year old, sometimes two years. This milk looks to the mother like free food, and the practice may not be bad if the mother is strong and healthy, and gives solid food as well, but it is disastrous in the case of undernourished mothers and weak babies. So we warn the mothers that they must start the babies eating early in life. We also keep a strict watch on the attendance and the weight charts. If the baby is not putting on weight, we have to find the reason, and in one or two cases we have admitted babies here as in-patients, with their mothers, to have special feeding. If any mother does not attend regularly, and gives no good reason, we stop giving milk, as it is clear that she is now able to manage without it."[8]

Dora enjoyed having children around the campus, and there were usually a few child in-patients who, as soon as they were well enough, roamed about in a merry and mischievous band. Seva Nilayam offered a much-needed service in referring children born with deformities such as hare lip, cleft palate and club foot (often the result of marriages between close family members) to a sympathetic surgeon in Madurai. They also admitted children with skin diseases or dreadful burns so they could have daily dressings in a clean environment.

---

[8] *Milk 1974*

Yet Dora was aware of the limitations imposed by local village conditions:

"... there are many difficulties in applying the benefits of medical technology in the villages. People who have to go on rocky roads or to step in mud and water find it impossible to use special shoes or calipers. They would rather go barefoot, even if they limp badly. Wheelchairs are not practicable in narrow cobbled streets or sandy lanes. Institutions where special help can be given are far apart and a suitable one may be in another state where a different language is spoken. Mothers of small children suffering from blindness or the effects of polio are not willing to let them out of their care at an early age, when they could benefit most from skilled teaching.

"Access to ordinary medicine is now much easier than it was when we first came here. There are more doctors and hospitals and bus transport reaches to surprisingly remote places. But it is still not much easier to surmount the difficulties connected with the care of the handicapped. Vellore Hospital, about 300 miles from Madurai, is famous for physiotherapy and rehabilitation of the disabled. So it was to Vellore that we sent one of our patients, Alagar, a young man who had his spine broken in a bus accident. He was unable to stand or walk a step. He had bedsores and needed long treatment before he was even able to go to hospital. When we sent him to Vellore, his mother and brother went, and took a room nearby so that they could take turns to wait on him by day and night. Alagar responded so well to treatment and showed such courage and perseverance that during his last month in hospital the doctor asked his relatives to leave, so that he could become quite self-reliant. He can now walk with crutches and calipers and is learning to become a tailor. He went through a tailoring course in the hospital and now he has an electric sewing machine which he can use at home.

"We are trying to care for a girl of ten who has a very rare condition of loss of sensation in the feet. It was thought at first that she had leprosy, as this disease causes loss of sensation, but tests proved that she has not. But the slightest injury to the feet causes deep ulcers and she has already lost some of her toes and must always wear special shoes. As she must have some indoor occupation, we have sent her to a hospital where she has stayed for some months; and besides having treatment for her ulcers, she has been taught to read and write. We are hoping to find a place where she can continue her education and also learn some useful trade or handicraft. She belongs to a family of the *dhobi* (washerman) caste but she can never follow that occupation which entails standing in stony streams and river beds to beat out the clothes. We have not yet found a place for her but are making enquiries.

"Another patient is a little boy who was horribly burned when a kerosene lamp fell on him from a shelf. His scars are healed, but he needs long and difficult plastic surgery. In the intervals between operations he stays with us and has an active merry life with the other child patients, so he is overcoming what must have been a shockingly traumatic experience. We hope that in time his features will be made sufficiently normal so that he will not suffer from a life-long handicap."[9]

There is a deep concern, affection and kindliness in the way Dora writes about the child care given in the clinic. Of course, she never had children of her own, but she was a mother and grandmother to many. She was by no means sentimental or unrealistic, but there is a compassion that shines through the Letters:

"Many mothers bring very sick babies, and it is easy to see, by every shade of expression on the mother's face, by the way she sits, and holds the baby, whether her anxiety is really deep, or whether she is one of those too poor, or tired, or slatternly mothers, who hope the baby will live, but are not prepared to exert themselves too much, and want some sort of magic medicine which will cure it.

"Other mothers bring babies who seem to have very little the matter with them, perhaps only a tiny sore. The baby is fat and jolly, and the mother bright and bold. The mother will bring out all kinds of complaints; the baby is not growing well, vomits the milk, has diarrhoea, is restless at nights. Yet it looks the picture of health. You don't believe her, and she knows that you don't. But she likes to have the baby looked at: it is pleasant and reassuring, she is getting a second opinion and she has the satisfaction of showing off the baby. If we went by her words alone, the baby might be dosed with all sorts of unnecessary medicines. A little conversation and fun, to which Tamil people always respond, fit the case better.

"But we can also see tormenting fear in the eyes of some

---

9 *Helping the Handicapped 1982*

mothers. Perhaps it is a first baby, perhaps an only baby because the husband is dead, and it is all she has in the world.

"She has worried herself sick, imagining that it is not growing, that its breathing is not normal, or there is something wrong with its eyes. It would be so easy just to give a few vitamin tablets and tell her not to worry. But if we want to allay these fears, we must spend some time with her. We can weigh the baby and tell the mother to come back in a week's time and see that it has put on weight. We must look at it very carefully, without any suggestion of haste or inattention; we may sound the heart and lungs with the stethoscope and assure her that all is well within. We must examine the mother also, and if she is anaemic, or debilitated, we must give her appropriate medicine, and explain that only if she looks after her own health will her milk be good for the baby."[10]

In *What Kind of Medicine?* Dora is at pains to point out how the simplicity, carefulness and frugality of their approach is not only appropriate but effective, and she never tires of celebrating the resilience of ordinary people:

"In India there is an immense variety of culture, tradition, religion and occupation, and to work in the clinic is to be thrown into the stream of this complex society. There are field workers, women with faded saris and men with torn shirts or none. The hands always tell the truth of this. There are moderately well-off farmers, who have put on a clean ironed shirt to come. There are women from semi-tribal villages, with impressive ornaments and beads. There are weavers, generally poor, and tired with too long

[10] *Looking at People 1980*

sitting at the loom. There are Muslim women shrouded in white, and old pious Hindus who make a meagre living doing ceremonies at the temples. There are young girls carefully shepherded by their mothers, and naked children running about in freedom. In time, anyone working in the clinic develops a sixth sense regarding the condition, status, and thoughts of all these people. Many people in the West today regret the passing of the old Family Doctor. We would like to be the Family Doctor to this particular patch of rural India.

"Ours is not a gleaming modern hospital, with up-to-date appliances and furniture. Our examination tables were made from packing cases. Our sterilising is done in a steamer on a kerosene stove. Our bandages are made from torn sheets collected by friends, and sent from England, Australia and Denmark. There are two reasons for working on this level. One is that we need all available money for medicines, and the other is that we believe that for our kind of treatment unnecessary complexity is a hindrance. People who have never been in a hospital, or those who have been in one, and have been frightened by its size and strangeness, do not hesitate to come to a place which feels more like home to them; with children, especially, we wish to keep the frightening aspects to the very minimum.

"We have found, over a period of twelve years, that our approach has been successful. We have found, also, in spite of hardship, neglect and malnutrition, that these people have remarkable powers of recovery, and we believe that medicine should encourage the body to heal itself in every way possible."[11]

But on occasions people arrived at the clinic too late. In one of her most profound and moving newsletters, Dora describes the death of a young woman and her simple funeral:

"The letter I wrote about our baby clinic was a happy one. In spite of all trials and anxieties we can see the result of our work, in the faces of babies eager to live, to love and be loved, and to find out about the world into which they have come.

"But sometimes, with that sense of life and hope still in my mind, I have to think about the end of the journey. People ask me: 'Does anyone die in your clinic. If so, what do you do?'

"As we have only a simple country clinic, we do not aim to take very serious cases, or those whose lives are in danger. We must try to get such patients into adequately equipped hospitals and, as no ambulances ever come here, we often have to help the patients' families in their transport difficulties. But we know very well that most people would choose to die in their homes, surrounded by their relatives, rather than in a hospital bed. Usually, those who feel that they have fulfilled their lives accept death easily, and would not want to go to extraordinary lengths to preserve a spark of life when further existence has no meaning.

"An individual life, dear though it may be, is like a ripple on an ever-moving stream. Very long ago, in the morning of the world, the Hindu scriptures, the *Upanishads*,

---

[11] *What Kind of Medicine?*

135

reached out to two great beliefs – that every human action brings its inescapable results, and that the world we see is not the ultimate reality. The prayer used at the time of death says: 'Ashes are my body's end... O mind, remember Brahman. O mind, remember thy past deeds.' And there is a much-used Sanskrit invocation:

Lead me from the unreal to the real;
Lead me from darkness to light;
Lead me from death to
immortality.[12]

"This does not mean that there is no mourning. Women, especially, are by custom obliged to take part in ritual lamentation, beating their breasts and crying to the dead one: 'Why did you go? Why do you leave us inconsolable?' But, at the same time, there is a very matter-of-fact side to funerals. The men of the house and the neighbours get together and bring bamboo poles to make a bier. A large coconut leaf, platted like a mat, is laid on these. Someone goes to the market, and buys a new cloth, white for a man, or a splendidly coloured sari for a woman, and the body is covered and garlanded with fresh flowers. Incense sticks are lighted. When all is ready, the bier is lifted, and carried to the burning ground. In the house, at the place where the body has lain, a lamp is lit, and garlands are placed there.

"It has happened to us a number of times to have to arrange a funeral. Patients may come to the clinic in a state of collapse. They have used all their strength to get here, and can get no farther. We are obliged to try to find

---

[12] *The Last Journey 1976*

the family, but it may be a hopeless quest. This is an area surrounded by mountains, where there are plantations of tea, coffee, cardamoms and citrus fruits. In the dry season there is not enough work on the plains, but in the rainy, misty mountains there is more work and better pay. If there is illness or death in the family it may be impossible to get in touch with someone who has gone looking for work.

"Some patients, tired of struggling with poverty and ill-health simply leave their homes and wander off, believing that they may somehow, somewhere, find a better a place. But it may be too late. There was one old woman who said: 'I would know how to get to my house but I don't know any address. I can't tell you where it is.' We sent someone to enquire at the village we thought was hers, but no one knew of her. It may not even have been the right village.

"A young girl, who looked about sixteen, came to us in a critical condition. She was severely anaemic, due to hook worm, her heart was failing, and her breathing laboured. Her face was so swollen that I doubt if anyone who knew her could have recognised her. But no one knew her. We gave her the best treatment we could, yet knowing it was hopeless. Even if an ambulance had by some miracle drawn up at the gate, she could not have lasted out the forty-five miles to hospital – the only hospital with blood transfusions to spare. Before evening she died.

"There are some local castes and communities who practise burial and not cremation, and it is easier for us to follow this custom. We sent for the cobblers, who are also the traditional grave diggers, and they went two hundred yards up the road, to the barren and thorny piece of ground which serves for funerals. While they are digging, we removed her old rags, washed the body and wrapped it in a clean white sheet. The girls wove a garland from the garden flowers. We lit the lamps and burned the incense; it was dusk before all was ready. No one followed the bier but the grave-diggers and our clinic staff; no one saw us on the road but some children playing by the door of a hut. The last light lingered on the hills. The lanterns shone on the faces of the men as they threw earth upon the body.

"Among all the funerals I have seen in my life, including state funerals of important persons, not one lives in my memory so vividly as this poor funeral of an unknown, ignorant girl. There was no place for sentimentality, for hypocrisy or empty show. Only one life gathered to the eternal unknown."

Chapter 10

SMALL IS BEAUTIFUL –
WORKING ON A HUMAN SCALE

We live in a world of limitations, but man alone thinks he can have expansion without limit, and continual gain without loss.
This fallacy is at the basis of many ills of the modern world ...

In Dora's Letters a "steady vision" runs like a golden thread throughout: service to the poorest, without distinction of class, caste or creed, simple, frugal living, the relief of suffering and the putting aside of self. The Letters demonstrate how she put her ideas into practice. As it says on her tomb, "Work is Love Made Visible".

She was very fond of E F Schumacher's writings. The name of her Handicraft Training Centre, *Good Work*, also acknowledges his influence. In the 1980s Dora made a trip to Rajasthan and returned with a group of Rajasthani metalworkers who created a "Persian Wheel" to draw water from the well. They spent a long time at Seva Nilayam fashioning the buckets that were lowered on a chain into the well and drawn up by a team of bullocks walking in a circle. As an example of Schumacher-style intermediate technology, it was remarkable, and Dora wrote admiringly of the skill and craftsmanship of these artisans. Yet the experiment was a failure. Dora blamed the inability of the local bullocks to learn to walk in a circle, when they had been used for many years to walk up and down a slope; but in reality, the water level fell too far, out of reach of the buckets and chain; and the electricity supply to the pump improved, so the Persian Wheel fell into disuse. Not all 'appropriate' technology was appropriate.

Dora was contemptuous of people who raised money by heart-rending accounts of poverty and destitution, making Indians out to be helpless victims. She celebrated the resilience of the Indian poor, as in this story of the 1979 cyclone:

"[A] young man had put up a small shop to sell tea, sweets, biscuits and sundries to passers-by, many of them patients coming to our clinic. This man is a good friend of ours and as he was not able to do heavy work because of ill health, we had encouraged him in this venture. We had been present at the little opening ceremony which is held according to custom with worship, camphor lights and offerings of fruit and flowers.

"The shop, like many on the roadsides of South India, was a portable one; it was brought here on a bullock cart. It was like a large box on legs, with a pitched roof and a door which could be closed. And now, when trade was just getting under way, a tree fell exactly on the shop, crushing it like a matchbox.

"But there was no weeping and wailing. Our staff and friends gathered round to see what could be salvaged. Amazingly, the copper tea urn and the glasses were brought out undamaged, having been protected in a little hollow under the shop. Tins of sweets and biscuits were found safe. A tarpaulin was stretched across some poles and the shop was soon open for business. The copper urn steamed merrily and probably more customers came than would have visited the undamaged shop.

"The cost of such a wooden box shop is about two hundred rupees (£12-13 [in 1979]), and with a loan from us the proprietor soon bought a new one. Many patients come into our clinic, get their number in the line, then go back for cups of tea and a chat.

"There are a great number of such people in India, people who meet adversity with courage and resourcefulness and are virtually unsinkable."[13]

Dora preferred to work "on the basis that the people are equal human beings with ourselves"; true compassion, she explains, consists in "helping people turn a difficult corner" not in trying to do everything for them, somehow making them our property and taking the credit if they do well. "Supposing they do not do well?" she asks. On the subject of poverty you can hear her dry humour come through: "Someone has said that poverty is a state of mind rather than a physical condition. To this, it might seem justifiable to answer 'Only try living on an Indian coolie's wages for a few months and then say if poverty is a state of mind'."

She explains the human scale approach to charity, how "statistics play a small part in our work", how careful consideration of each person's needs should be the criterion: "how much easier to dole out milk powder to all comers, and take a photo of a ring of smiling faces!" and this careful consideration comes from knowing how people live and what their challenges are. "It is so easy if you see a child with a torn frock, and you have some material, to give a new one – why not? But next day there will be ten children with torn frocks, or no frock at all, all demanding clothes: then there will be trouble and bad feeling." She often wrote about the folly of westerners sponsoring a particular child: "Think what trouble that would cause in the village!"

---

[13] *The Cyclone 1979*

The simplicity of her life at Seva Nilayam harks back to her Liverpool home, her Devon cottage and smallholding, her apartment in Budapest and her dwelling in Mudichur; rather than feeling it is deprivation, it is a liberation. To Alison Selford, reporting a visitor's complaint about the bathrooms at Seva Nilayam, she retorts:

"I would not change our bathrooms for any bathrooms I have been in in Europe. Ours are just walls, open to the sky. You bathe in a chequered pattern of light and shade from the leaves of the coconut palm, and looking up you see a bunch of bananas ripening above your head. Even if it rains, it isn't cold rain, and it's delightful to bathe in the rain."

Living simply, without luxuries, close to local conditions, allows you to understand how your patients have to live. This she felt some missionaries failed to do, to the detriment of their work:

"It is irritating (to me and must be to Indians) to see the missionaries going round in their cars, with bouncing sons and daughters, fresh from healthy schools in the hill station, with flasks of cold drinks, lunches in plastic boxes, and lots of fruit.

"How could such people understand the trials of life on day wages, with little food, and poor living conditions?

"In the world today it is often easier to be big than small. Very often, the money is there; materials, technique and workers can be provided. If you can be big, why be small? You can reach more people, you can do more good.

"Can you? In fact, you cannot. After a certain point in

growth you begin to lose something. You are seduced by plans and figures, gadgets and luxuries, all in the name of saving the world from poverty and pain. You can lose your discrimination, your sensitivity, your compassion.

"... It is not possible to define the point at which we begin to lose direction. For every step on the road there is a good excuse. This will save time, that will make life more comfortable, something else will enable us to start some new activity. Improvements are not wrong and there is no virtue as such in anything that is tumbledown or worn out. So how can we decide our course? Only by discrimination, and a steady vision of our first inspiration, using this as a touchstone in any decision."[14]

A commitment to human scale technology meant that Dora determinedly sought out the Government-sponsored khadi shops, these days rather dwarfed by huge and glittering factory-made textile shops, to buy handloom cloth for presents at festival time. Gandhi always advocated handloom weaving as a means of supporting local cottage industries for rural self-sufficiency. But the value of making things with the hands has a deeper significance: Dora recalls the experience of her cousin, Mary Osborn, who met Gandhi when he visited England. Gandhi himself taught her to spin and she went on to create a centre, the Stanton Guildhouse in the Cotswolds, dedicated to creativity, learning and personal development. Although the cousins lost touch, they reconnected in the 1980s and Mary Osborn travelled to India to stay at Seva Nilayam. She recalls this meeting in her book, *Stone upon Stone*, and it must have been a remarkable encounter:

---

[14] *Small is Beautiful 1978*

"This was a wonderful moment for us both, as we had not met since we were very young, our lives having taken us geographically in quite different directions. Yet when we talked that evening, we discovered how closely our ideals and aspirations were in tune."

Dora made a habit of travelling on the local bus, and always resisted offers of a vehicle for Seva Nilayam. (Before the leprosy hospital started near Aundipatti, the mobile leprosy clinic used to go out in a bullock cart, which shows some dedication on the part of the staff, but also realism, as there were many roads in those days impassable by motor vehicles, but navigable by cart). Dora makes a virtue of using public transport, enjoying the bustle of the bus stand, meeting friends and drinking tea while she waited for the bus:

"... people appreciate the fact that we travel with them, and talk to them. They help to hoist our bags of provisions and boxes of medicines on to the bus; mothers show their babies, and ask if they can get medicine from our clinic; they are curious about what we have got in our shopping bags. Bus manners allow you to mind other people's business as well as your own."

The stately coconut trees were one of the first things planted on Seva Nilayam land. They form part of a holistic rural economy based on locally available resources:

"... nuts are very far from being all the trees produce. The coconut has a distinctive way of growing: as the trunk lengthens, the lower leaves fall off, and only the upper leaves remain to form the graceful head which sways in the breeze. The leaf stalks are surprisingly strong and heavy, and are a source of firewood. The leaf is divided into many long and narrow leaflets, and the central ribs of these, when shredded out and tied together, make brooms of just the right flexibility for the work they have to do. Every day all the paths are swept, as well as the area in front of the clinic, which has been crowded with patients in the morning. The clinic floors are cleaned by water being poured freely on them and swept out with brooms. Further, the coconut leaves, when plaited, are used for thatch, and at any time we can put up a pandal – a roof to give extra shade – or a small hut, at practically no cost. Still further, part of the leaf stem, when soaked in water, and mashed at one end with a hammer, makes a most effective whitewash brush.

"All this shredding and plaiting of leaves is done by patients or local people, while they sit together in a social group. This is the way people have lived and worked in the village from time immemorial. The ease with which useful things can be obtained makes it possible for the poorest people to spend most of their money on food and clothes, and very little on household articles. Clay pots, of beautiful shape and rich red-brown colour, are made by the village potter, and are very cheap. All the leaves that are swept up are used for compost, and all the fallen branches for firewood. But I find that villagers can always give one a lesson in economy. One day I had some rather thorny branches which I thought could well be burnt up. But as I was setting light to them two women who were passing said: 'Don't do that, give them to us', and they took them home to cook the supper."[15]

"In South India you cannot travel very far or eat many meals without encountering the banana leaf. It is spread

---

[15] *How Far Will the Money Go?* 1974

145

before you as a plate and used to wrap food you buy to carry away. On the trains you buy curd rice, lemon rice, or tamarind rice made into a packet with a banana leaf. At weddings the guests seated in rows on mats are each furnished with a banana leaf from which to feast.

"At a small country restaurant I finished my meal, and according to custom, picked up my leaf and carried it to the hand-washing place. As I put the leaf down the small chute I saw two big eyes, a sniffing muzzle and a questing tongue. The proprietor's cow was waiting for the leaves to come through, and finding them very succulent in spite of the remains of chutney or pickles adhering to them.

"No figures can show the value of this 'banana leaf economy' to South India. It is not described in books or pamphlets or held up as a model of ecological conservation or re-cycling, but thousands of leaves must go to enrich the soil every day. The banana grows very quickly, and the young leaf, when unrolled, is a beautiful clear pale green. The used leaves disintegrate quickly also and form a rich black nitrogenous fertilizer. North India is less fortunate than the South as bananas are scarcer outside the tropics and no other leaf has its advantages of sizeand ready availability; the plant grows at all seasons and produces fruit as well as leaves."[16]

One of Dora's passions was the Kapok, or silk-cotton tree. It is a curious tree, she writes, its bare branches covered with dry looking pods which are full of silky hairs and seeds the size of peppercorns. It grows well even in dry places and, with a little persuasion and tenacity, involving some very basic technology,

---

[16] *The Banana Leaf Economy 1983*

it produces useful materials:

> "Kapok is one of the treasures of South India. The staple is not long enough for it to be spun and woven, but it can be made into quilts, pillows, cushions and padded jackets. You may ask why quilts and padded jackets are useful in a tropical country, but where mountains rise to seven thousand feet the climate becomes quite cold. The mid-day sun can be warm but temperatures may drop almost to freezing point at night. The smooth silk fibres do not clog or become lumpy, and a kapok quilt may even be washed, if care is taken to turn and shake it while drying.

> "When we first came to Seva Nilayam, we did not know anything about the kapok tree. We learned gradually. We found that we could make ourselves very comfortable with pillows and mattresses but we had not mastered the technique of getting the seeds out. We had to do it by twirling a stick with a wire cross on the end. After using the pillows for a time we found loose seeds accumulating in the corners. But we persevered and after several models with drums and revolving spikes we made the one which is in use at present and which we find quite satisfactory."[17]

The silk cotton is one of the main materials used in Dora's handicraft training centre. Using locally available materials, and local crafts and skills, they turned scraps of donated fabric and silk cotton from their own trees into saleable toys, quilts and jackets. These could be sold in the handicraft shop in the local hill station. Soft toys such as teddy bears were also produced although Dora often despaired of getting the expression on the

---

[17] *As Soft as Silk 1986*

bear's face quite right.

In an early fragment of writing she notes that she was an ecologist before the term was well-known. She knows about limits to growth and the penalties, rather than the economies, of scale; she comes across as a systems thinker, seeing the deep connections between small actions and the way they ripple out into the wider world. Her philosophy and beliefs, shaped by the events of her long life, found expression in an authenticity of relationships with the human and natural world in which she found an endless source of fascination and delight.

Chapter 11

SOUTH INDIAN VILLAGE LIFE
AND TRADITIONS

People see a thatched hut, no furniture, primitive cooking arrangements, small shops, long journeys, bare feet, dusty roads, and they think how they would feel if they had to live like this, but the people who are living it don't feel like that at all. It is normal life, and full of interest and excitement.

*B*irds of an Indian Village, written in Mudichur, is a celebration of the "brilliant plumage, strong personalities and interesting habits" of local birds, and documents the interdependence of people and wildlife: the kites swooping down to steal from people fishing in the pond, the vivid green bee-eaters using her fence for a perch, the drongo (a bird of omens: "people will alter their plans, and put off their business if the drongo says that the time is not auspicious"); riding on the back of a buffalo. There is a keenly observed portrait of the hoopoes nesting in her building: "it was a fine sight to see first one, then the other fly down from the roof, each raising and lowering its crest on touching the ground."

After creating and protecting a garden around her little house, ("after only one rainy season, the place began to take on an embowered, secluded look"), she hears:

"... a new bird-voice ... a vigorous and happy song, with a kind of bubble in it, recalling clear springs and runnels of water. It was the bul-bul ... a handsome bird, with a slightly crested, perky black head, a brown-grey body, and a brilliant patch of pure scarlet under the tail. When he

149

came, I knew certainly that I had a garden, and not a mere patch of ground in the wilderness. But most thrilling was the arrival of the purple sunbird. These tiny creatures are only a little bigger than hummingbirds, and like hummingbirds they suck honey from flowers, and can feed in this way while hovering. They flit about the trees and bushes, scarcely distinguishable from flowers themselves, all lightness, eagerness and joy. ... The male is black, with an iridescent purple sheen; the female has a brown back and clear primrose-yellow breast. They built a nest at the utmost tip of a long swinging trail of bougainvillea. It was a tiny soft pouch of fine grass, tastefully ornamented on the outside with scraps of paper and caterpillar droppings. It had a little overhanging porch, and under this the curved beak of the hen- bird showed as she sat, steadfast and unperturbed while the frail pouch swung in every breeze.

"There is nothing, no, nothing at all, to match the sweetness of a spring evening in England, after rain, when the blackbird calls and calls as though nothing could ever stop him. And Indian birds may be splendid, and their voices pleasing, or harsh; they do not sing so as to hold you to the spot, listening for that voice again and again; they do not touch the heart. So I thought, but I forgot one exception. One evening, I heard a clear 'pe-lo-lo' through the trees. It was the golden oriole. He is the cousin of the blackbird, and his voice has the same pure music, untouched by any shrillness or brashness, any chirps or twitters. But as if to show that colour and song can go together, he is, apart from his black head and wings, a rich canary yellow. 'Pe-lo-lo, pe-lo-lo, pe-lo-lo' he sang, and I saw the golden gleam.

... How should he have come to a scorched village on the

plains? But for a few minutes he must have found my garden alluring. 'Pe-lo-lo, pe-lo-lo, pe-lo-lo' came his sweet voice, and I could not but feel it a triumph that he should sing here at all – even though the next minute he was gone, and my garden was silent again."

It is hard to imagine Dora setting up her typewriter in her Keeraipothampatty hut, yet numerous articles were dispatched to Alison for hopeful distribution to publishers. In one essay, entitled *Bread,* she (unusually) recalls her life in Hungary and a friend, Mrs. Horvath, whose breakfast table was a feast for Dora, not only of good bread but also of Hungarian tales. She contrasts the sacred nature of rice in India with the rich traditions of bread-making in Europe, and concludes with a cry from the heart:

"I would like to show these people something of the way we in Europe imagine things; how we have had our dreams and our awakenings; how much striving, how much sorrow, how much heroism and how much cruelty has made up the web of our history in this half century. But it is all so far away. The little things they understand – the proverbs that echo each other in many languages, the customs of seed-time and harvest. How can I make them understand what we suffered in the struggle for that freedom which is more than rice and more than bread?"

Dora admires the beauty and durability of kitchen vessels:

"Over the centuries many a young bride has gone out proudly to fetch water for the home, many an old woman looks back on long years of water carrying without knowing when it will end, or a little girl is eager to put a water pot on her head because it makes her feel grown up. All the pots return to dust, but new ones must constantly be made. The rival of the clay pot is the brass vessel of the same shape which is given as a wedding present. It is heavier, of course, and makes work more laborious, but it will outlast generations of clay pots. It is valuable property and many great old houses have an immense array of brass vessels of all sizes and ages, some only to be used at special festivals. The polished brass pot can strike sparkles from the early sunlight as it goes to the well, and we can imagine it looking down on the humble clay pot, which comes from the wheel today but may lie in fragments a few months or years hence. The brass pot is a symbol of the family's wealth and stability but it can even be pawned in time of need."[18]

Then there is the skilled work of the village potter: the choosing of the clay, the hand-turned wheel, the laborious firing process.

Dora celebrates many of the traditional skills in daily use:

"The basket makers sit just in the street, or under an improvised awning if the weather is hot. No one pauses to admire the skill and dexterity or the sure and rapid movements of their fingers.

"There is another variation of the basket work, the marram. A triangular tray peculiarly shaped, deeper at the broad end and with an opening at the narrow end. It is made of split bamboo and is used for winnowing grain or cleaning it. With a movement that combines tossing, and shaking, a woman can separate broken rice from whole grains, or separate two kinds of grain which have

---

[18] *The Brass Pot and the Clay Pot 1990*

become accidentally mixed or extract unwanted grains and weed seeds. Let anyone not accustomed to such work try this, and they will admit it requires a very high degree of skill."[19]

She admires the skills of the humble shoe mender; the expertise of the field workers who can level a rice field to a completely flat sheet of shimmering water; the *dhobi* (washerman): "Dhobis have their secrets and it is truly remarkable to see that they can bring the clothes dazzling white out of what sometimes looks a muddy pool". She spends hours waiting in bus stands and has many opportunities to observe the skill of the tea-shop owner:

"The tea and sugar are not mixed with a spoon but by being poured a number of times back and forth from one glass to another. The expert tea maker will raise his arm high over his head, and direct the stream of tea from a height of four feet into the second glass, held at hip level, without spilling a drop. This fine flourish ensures perfect mixing, and a slight cooling of the boiling tea. A real artist may follow it up by skimming a spoonful of the creamy froth from the milk, dropping it on top of the tea, and lightly dusting it with sugar."[20]

As persons of some standing in the community, Dora and her team were often invited to weddings. She paints a vivid picture:

"Village houses are not large enough to hold a wedding party, so a pandal, a temporary roof, has to be made outside. This is made with poles and plaited coconut

---

[19] *Unvalued Assets 1984*
[20] *A Good Cup of Tea 1984*

leaves, or sometimes with saris lent for the occasion. They are semi-transparent, and the light below the pandal is tinted with rose or green or violet. In this case, the whole lane had been roofed over, and a few benches and string cots put out for the guests to sit on.

"The lane was crowded. There were many children carrying babies, little brothers or sisters, as in India they love to do. The children were dressed in their best, but even ragged and dirty children were not kept out. The bride went in procession through the village, with a retinue of women carrying baskets and dishes of fruit, grain and new clothes as presents. Then bride and groom sat together on a bench with downcast eyes and serious faces. The guests may laugh and chatter as they will, but the bride, especially, must be serious, or she may be thought to be light-minded. Both bride and groom wore garlands of roses, and the bride's hair was beautifully dressed with jasmine flowers.

"Three dishes, of different grains, were placed on the ground before the couple. The local priest led off by sprinkling a little of each grain on the couple. Then the parents and near relatives followed, then neighbours, friends and well-wishers. Each one stretched out hands three times in blessing towards the couple, and many of the hands so extended were rough and wrinkled with toil. Many of the old women who came had not even a new sari for the occasion, but there was a warmth and intensity about the ceremony which was very moving. And, as I noticed, at the end all the grain was carefully swept into a cloth, to be sifted and used.

"The actual marriage consists in a threefold exchange of

garlands between the bride and groom, and then the tying, by the groom, of the *thali*, a gold or saffron cord bearing an amulet placed round the bride's neck. This she will always wear proudly as the sign of her married state. At the moment of marriage there is a roll of drums and the guests throw jasmine flowers and coloured rice over the couple, and good upbringing of a son or daughter is crowned, for the parents, by the selection of a worthy marriage partner. This is their reward and privilege. Not all the marriages go well, it is true, but the West, with its millions of broken homes, cannot claim that free choice ensures happiness."[21]

Village festivals were important milestones in Seva Nilayam's year, and as Dora acknowledges, "People need an excuse for merrymaking, so that they can spend a bit extra and stay off work without reproaching themselves for being lazy or extravagant. On the contrary; it is meritorious to keep festivals well." Most important for Tamils is the Pongal festival in mid-January:

"The rains are over, cool weather has come, days are serene and sunny, and dew falls in the silence of the starry nights. There is a feeling of having come into some quiet place from which troubles have receded into the far distance. It is hard now to imagine the burning heat of May, the cutting winds and raging dust storms of July, the empty wells and the parched fields. Nature has grown wealthy and kind.

"The paddy fields turn from green to pale gold. The rice is harvested, and everyone is out in the fields, cutting, threshing and stacking. Sometimes we thresh the grain by

[21] *A Country Wedding 1983*

moonlight; four pairs of bullocks tread the sheaves, going round in a circle while the workers throw more and more sheaves under their feet, and excited children shout and play.

"In October, we sowed pumpkin seeds, and the plants have ramped over all the available space, even climbing trees, where the ripening fruits hang like huge orange moons. They will be ready for our Pongal feast.

"Yes, we must be ready by the fourteenth of January. Every building must be whitewashed inside and out; all the damage of the past year must be repaired, and many cottages are painted with freehand designs, or with the auspicious red and white stripes. At other times it may be difficult to persuade busy workers to spend time and energy on whitewashing, but at Pongal it is done spontaneously; there is no need to ask. Quicklime is fetched from the bazaar, and brushes made by hammering and fraying out the stems of coconuts. When the whitewashing is finished the floors are decorated with traditional *kolam* patterns done with white powder.

"Pongal is the chief harvest festival of South India. It lasts three days. People buy new pots and baskets, and for weeks the village potter has been busy making clay pots and large storage jars. On the first night of Pongal a bonfire is made of all the worn-out mats, brooms and baskets, before the new ones are taken into use.

"The second day is the great feast. Everyone, even if poor, tries to have new clothes. At Seva Nilayam we give a present to each of the friends who have helped us during the past year, the neighbours and their children, our clinic staff and field workers, the washerman, the tailor, the barber, and some poor families round about.

"No one sleeps very much. The cooking goes on all night; it is a communal task, and all the women lend a hand. There is no room for it indoors, so it is done outside under a trellis covered with climbing gourds.

"A fireplace is improvised with large stones, and the fire is fed with sticks and brushwood. Piles of vegetables are cut and rice is boiled in a great brass vessel. Even those who sleep are astir by daybreak, bathed and wearing their new clothes. By about ten-thirty in the morning the feast is ready. It consists of a special *pongal* - sweet rice, plain rice with spiced vegetables, green beans and sweet pumpkin, followed by *payasam*, a sweet made from tapioca, cashew nuts and raisins, delicately flavoured with cardamoms. Mats are spread on the floor, and the diners sit down on these, each with a freshly cut banana leaf for a plate. There will be at least three relays of feasters, including ragged children from the lane, cleaned and tidied up for once. It is always a delight to see rows of children sitting in the dappled shade of the trellis, eating their fill. The food is simple enough, being mainly our own produce, but it is well cooked, and served with care. In the afternoon the cooks make up for lost sleep, and others rest or play as they feel inclined.

"The third day of Pongal is dedicated to the cattle. Our beautiful white cart bullocks are scrubbed clean, and their horns are oiled. They do no work, and all the animals have a special feed. All, right down to the newest calf, wear flower garlands. The cart has been freshly painted, and a ceremony with camphor lights and incense is carried out in front of it.

"Near the cowshed a fire is lighted, and a pot of sweet, milky rice is boiled. It must boil over, as a symbol of plenty, and then all shout 'Pongal O! Pongal O!' The rice is shared out, and eaten with bananas and pieces of sugar cane.

"I think it is good to have festivals which remind us of all those things we depend on for our living. Cattle are the mainstay of India. If a supernatural power wanted to disrupt the country totally the quickest way would be to get rid of all the bullocks. We can survive stoppages on the railways, cuts in electricity, breakdown of the telegraph system, lack of kerosene and of buses – indeed all these have happened since we have been at Seva Nilayam – but without the bullocks we would be lost."[22]

Other festivals are also lovingly described at length:

"In October we have a festival which seems to me one of the most beautiful, and its underlying thought can be shared by people of any religious belief or none. It is Ayudha Puja, the day when each one pays honour to the tools of his trade. The carpenter brings his saw and chisel, the clerk or teacher his pen and books, the mason his trowel. I always find it moving to see the worn and dented spades which have been used day in, day out, in the mud washed and decorated, and laid before the images of the Gods. We don't make a division between ancient and modern, as if only old things were worthy; the sewing machine, the microscope in the clinic, and the irrigation

---

[22] *Pongal 1976*

pump are decorated with flowers. Man is offering his work, whatever it is, as the best gift he has.

"At Seva Nilayam, in our tropical climate, we have flowers in the garden every day of the year – scarlet and orange hibiscus, jasmine, cannas, cassias, frangipani and bougainvillea. So decorations are easy, and the rest of the materials, coloured powders, and incense sticks, cost only a little in the bazaar.

"In November comes the festival of Deepavali. Before man understood why the sun seemed to retreat and the days grow shorter towards the end of the year, he felt he must do something to assert this hope and belief that the darkness would be only transitory. With us, in South India, the shortening of the days is not pronounced; there is only a variation of an hour or so between June and December. But the darker days come at the same time as the onset of the North East Monsoon, which brings towering clouds and majestic thunderstorms. Deepavali, in mid-November, is a festival of light. It may be raining – indeed, it should be, for rain here is longed for. When it rains you see smiling faces, and people wade cheerfully through mud and water even if they have no raincoats and very few have umbrellas.

"Deepavali is the time for fireworks, and stalls appear in the local bazaar and the streets of Madurai, selling Catherine wheels, red and green flares, fire fountains, jumping crackers, sparklers, writhing snakes, and somehow keeping them dry. They are small-scale fireworks and setting them off is a domestic occasion. Seva Nilayam invites the poor children from round about.

"Deepavali is also an occasion for new clothes. At Seva Nilayam we have about thirty in-patients and workers on the farm. We manage to provide something for all, and also for neighbours who have been helpful, and some very poor families. We start saving up clothes many months before; some come from parcels sent by Friends of Seva Nilayam; some are made by the village tailor, and some picked up as bargains from travelling salesmen or on shopping expeditions. So the cupboard slowly gets full.

"Before Deepavali it is a pleasure just to go to Madurai to see the crowds of shoppers. The cloth shops hang out displays of saris glowing with entrancing colours. Many shops close in the mid-day hours and stay open late in the evening. So the sunset light, usually in monsoon time a fiery glow, mingles with the lights of the shops, and clothes the moving crowd with splendour. Those who spend are happy, and those who sell are happy too, as they make a hard-earned profit, to which they have been looking forward for months. Those who have no shops sit on the pavement with pieces of cloth for blouses and skirts, with aluminium kitchen pots, fruits, mats, hair ornaments, towels, anything they can invest a little money in. Madurai is never so cluttered, never so good tempered so expectant and so glad.

"On the festival day, at Seva Nilayam, the children are up at four; they take their bath and put on their new clothes, and then they have their special breakfast of idlies – steamed rice cakes. And in the evening come the fireworks.

"What about Christmas? Where we live there are very few Christians, but Hindus are usually very ready to rejoice with all who keep their own festivals, believing that everyone has his own path, and finds help in his own way. No image of the Divine could be more acceptable in India than that of a mother and baby. Where there has in the past been fierce resistance to Christianity it was because those who became Christians were expected to repudiate all their own traditions and sacred symbols, and to believe these were of the Devil. But those days are over. So we keep Christmas. We have no pine or fir trees, but we can make garlands. We have sweets and fruits and every boy gets some glass marbles, and every girl some new bangles or hair ribbons.

"What of India's poverty? Can people be so happy? You would have to be at Seva Nilayam to see what joy can be given by glass marbles costing about twelve English pence a hundred. Or a breakfast of rice cakes. Or a sari of printed cotton. Or a shirt made out of dressmaker's pieces. It is one of the paradoxes of life that only those who know sorrow can truly know joy, and only those who are poor know what it is to feel rich."[23]

---

[23] *Festivals 1974*

Chapter 12

◆————◆————◆

TRAVELS

For to admire an' for to see,
For to be'old this world so wide –
It never done no good to me,
But I can't drop it if I tried.
(Rudyard Kipling)

Dora considered that the way she had travelled to India was the "right" way; and she never lost her love of the sea, despite eventually settling inland.

"When I came to India the sea passage was the normal way, and to fly was exceptional. It took fourteen days from Southampton to Colombo on the Dutch liner *Oranje* and I believe that this is undoubtedly the best way to enter a strange country. The life on shipboard gives you a chance to cut off gently from the land you have left, and to turn in thought to the land to which you are going. The voice of India calls: it is one voice made of a multitude of voices, and what they are you do not know. Meanwhile, there are so many experiences: opportunity to make new acquaintances and leisure to be alone; nights when you float between sea and stars, or watch the phosphorescent wake of the ship, a path of golden fire; days when you look for flying fish, and porpoises gambolling in the clear water. All across the Indian Ocean there is no land in sight, until at last you see the Laccadive Islands. They seem to consist only of a white lighthouse and some lines of coconut trees standing apparently in the water. Soon you will see Ceylon, the approach to India.

"If I want to recapture the spirit of the sea I can go down to the port of Madras. The old white-pillared Custom House looks much as it did a century ago. The sights and sounds of a seaport have much in common all the world over. Looking through the chasms between the tall buildings I can see the ocean, stretching to the horizon, indigo, with the catamarans, the primitive fishing boats, riding on it like specks, and the ships unloading their cargo with the rattle of chains and the creaking of ropes. The narrow streets of the port area are unbelievably congested. The huge bullocks pulling the drays give place to no- one, and make cars and scooters look small and ineffective, while the cycle rickshaws weave carelessly in and out of the mass of traffic. There are ancient solid warehouses which may date from the time of the East India Company, and here and there are mosques, temples and churches hemmed in between them. There are scents of coffee being roasted and spices being ground, there are noisy and crowded restaurants. There is the old Armenian Church, which has long been closed because the once flourishing community of Armenian merchants exists no more, but which still offers a place for reflection and quiet in the midst of all the noise, in its paved enclosure with fragrant white-flowered frangipani trees and well-watered plants. To be in a seaport stirs the imagination of all who love the sea."[24]

For Dora it was natural that when the opportunity arose, she would take off on travels around India, alone, or with Reddy, or with other companions, and this lasted well into

[24] *Down to the Sea in Ships 1985*

her eighties. Her inexhaustible curiosity about India made these travels a delight to her, although she is keen to keep away from the well- trodden routes: she was delighted to find Sanchi, in 1961, "agreeably quiet and free from all the riff-raff who pursue tourists at more visited places."

"It is true that there are still hundreds of thousands of devout believers, up and down India, who go alone, on foot, living sparely and on alms, meditating and seeking to understand the riddle of life. But for others, not wholly committed to such austerities, the distinction between pilgrimage and holiday is becoming blurred. We may want to see Tirupathi, one of the holiest shrines of South India, and we may take two or three days to do so, but we also get away from our daily cares, have a beautiful journey into the hills, eat, rest and enjoy ourselves as we please. The pilgrimage provides a focal point to a holiday."[25]

She took a journey with Reddy to the Himalayas to visit the shrine at Badrinath, joining with thousands of pilgrims:

"For more than a thousand years pilgrims have travelled the road from Hardwar, where the Ganges enters the plains of North India, to Badrinath, far up in the Himalayas, in the area in which many streams converge to form the mighty river. Badrinath is one of the holiest, remotest and least accessible of the shrines of India.

"For more than a thousand years pilgrims went on foot. Directions given earlier in this century say that the traveller must take a waterproof groundsheet, a sleeping bag, woollen clothes, leather boots and socks; he must

---

[25] *Holidays 1990*

have an injection against cholera and should take a kerosene stove. Potatoes could be bought on the way, but he must not expect fresh fruit or vegetables. But for centuries the pilgrim went with only a woollen shawl and leather sandals, a staff and a bowl.

"Now there is a bus route all the way and peaches, plums and small apples can be bought at roadside stalls and good food in village shops. Between September and May the road is closed, being blocked by snow, but from May to September it is possible to reach Badrinath within two days, with a night's rest half way. It has always seemed to me that a pilgrimage should entail some special effort or hardship, but I must confess that without the bus I should never have been able to go there.

"It was late July, and that is the rainy season. On the lower slopes the forest was green and dripping wet. Waterfalls splashed on to the bus and small landslips blocked the road with shale and gravel, which was hastily being cleared. After the first hundred miles we stayed for the night at a traveller's lodge, and set out the next morning in rain. But as the weather cleared, valley after valley opened up, each deeper and grander than the last. Far above, the heights were swathed and banded with mist; far below the streams roared through vertically cut gorges. We could look down on a tiny suspension bridge appearing no bigger than a toy, and realize with a thrill of fear that we had to cross it ... down, down, by fantastic bends and turns, and at last, after clattering across the bridge, up, up, by a similar number of bends.

"Above Jothimath there are no more trees. The heights rise bare and stark. A bitter wind is blowing as the bus turns into a broad valley, between jagged black peaks, snow crowned. The little town consists only of travellers' lodges and a few shops, which will all be closed and abandoned when the snow descends. We are at a height of ten-and-a-half thousand feet, and very near the Tibetan border.

"As dusk descends the bell chimes from the temple across the river; and worshippers flock there. Within the sanctuary a fire is kindled and brought out to be carried through the throng. It is light, pure light, symbol of the Eternal. The temple is dedicated to Vishnu, the Creator. The endearing legends of the Hindu gods, and semi-divine heroes, are left behind, in the face of One Reality.

"Shells embedded in the rocks of the highest Himalayas prove that the whole vast mountain range was once at the bottom of the sea. The limestone rocks were laid down through many millennia from the bodies of minute sea creatures. Then the whole mass was lifted by movements of the earth's crust, so powerful that the strata which were once horizontal may even be vertical.

"Indian philosophy sees the whole process as one of creation and destruction; and here it is happening before our eyes. Great slabs of rock split off and fall into the abyss. The streams are turbid with sand and silt, which is carried down to form the fertile soil of the Gangetic plain. The pebbles are rolled in the torrents till they are polished and round. Every day thousands of tons of debris must be carried down. The day we descend from the Himalayas they are already less than the day we ascended.

"Such is the grandeur that perhaps a thousand years will pass before there is any perceptible change in the outline.

But the process is inevitable. At the height of Badrinath we feel like the tiniest ants on the earth's surface, but in the light of eternity the mountains themselves are ephemeral.

"Perhaps in some remote age they will again be under the sea. Perhaps new ranges will arise in other regions. The mightiest mountains are ever-changing:

Like clouds they shape themselves and go."[26]

Dora's appreciation of and fascination with the diversity of Indian religious experience shines through the accounts of her travels.

"Jodhpur station is a very busy place. It is in Rajasthan, at the end of the green cultivated land, and the beginning of the desert which stretches away to the Pakistan border. Many races and tribes meet there, camel breeders from Jaisalmer, Marwari cloth merchants, businessmen representing companies exploiting the mineral wealth of Rajasthan, villagers going to a famous fair. When I was last there, this fair was in progress, and the station platform was dazzling with the costumes of Rajasthani and Bihari peasant women in holiday dress – yellow, orange, crimson and purple, with tinselled borders and filmy veils.

"At the same time a pilgrim train had halted just outside the station. This train tours many of the sacred places of India stopping for a few days at each. It offers no amenities besides hard wooden seats and berths, but it tours for three months, and the fare is amazingly low – one hundred and fifty Rupees (about £9, sterling, at the

---

[26] *Badrinath 1982*

current rate of exchange). The pilgrims wash their clothes and bathe at the station fountains, and the open space outside may be glowing with cooking fires as they bake their wheaten cakes on the side of mounds of hot ashes, and the sauce pot bubbles on top. The pilgrims will make their devotions at the temple, see all the sights, compare the local agriculture and the price of grains, oil and vegetables with their own, and have a good rest and sleep. As in medieval Europe, piety can be combined with a good deal of jollity, and the desire to travel can be provided with an acceptable aim.

"On the crowded station platform, where groups of fairgoers sat gossiping, and business men in neat cool shirts, carrying brief cases, stood drinking tea at the refreshment stall, I saw an old woman with a white sari drawn over her grey hair, sitting cross- legged, with erect back and bent head, rhythmically clapping together a pair of tiny brass cymbals, only two or three inches across, which are often carried by traveling holy men. She was doing her bhajan, worship with music, even though her music was only the clapping together of two small discs of brass. I could not hear, in the hubbub, whether she was singing softly, or just repeating holy names. No-one thought her at all strange, no one knocked against her in that swirling mass, all treated her with respect. This was her chosen way, and who could question it?

"To the Hindu, religion is not a set of dogmas to be asserted but a path to be followed. Every soul is known to the eternal and must pass from time to eternity. The path may be wild and rugged, or direct and peaceful. It may be full of deceptions and illusions; it may lead, as many think, through many incarnations, but the picture of the devout Hindu is always that of the seeker, the pilgrim from time to eternity.

"Perhaps this may not seem to square with what one sees in the city streets every day. 'Religion' can turn into conjuring tricks, self-advertisement or sheer begging, arousing either the credulous interest or the annoyance of tourists. Also there is a multiplicity of gods and a seemingly endless supply of legends about them. There is rivalry between the devotees of one god and another. There are local gods in the villages who are unknown to orthodox Hinduism.

"But God can be worshipped under many names and forms, each embodying some aspect of the one. Man is [27]body and spirit, not pure spirit only, and needs some material image as the centre of devotion. But there are those who have sought long and meditated long, and no longer need such a material image. There is the Sanskrit saying *neti, neti* "not this, not this" meaning that whatever we can think about God, it is so far from adequate as to be even, in a manner of speaking, untrue.

"One of the greatest Christian theologians, after spending a lifetime writing many volumes, at the end of his life said, 'All I have written is of as little value as straw'. An Indian philosopher would understand that."

The local hill station of Kodaikanal – with its "rocks full of moss and ferns, coffee, teak and eucalyptus plantations, oranges, pears, limes" - was a place of refuge in the hot weather and Dora had friends there with whom she could stay, enjoying blankets,

---

[27] *Many Paths 1982*

and log fires.

"Kodaikanal lies at an elevation of between six and seven thousand feet above sea level, with the highest peaks rising to nine thousand feet. In early days the ascent was very tedious. There were no roads, and while the men could ride on horseback, the women and children had to be carried in 'doolies,' litters slung between poles resting on the shoulders of bearers. The path was rough and zig-zag between towering rocks. Now, a winding but well-kept road ascends from Batlagundu and is used by buses, private cars, lorries and ponies. It passes, first, through deep forest, where monkeys swing from the trees, and, if you listen, you can hear the calls of many beasts and birds. Then there is an area of coffee plantations interspersed with bananas, jack fruit and oranges. Higher again are bare grasslands with thick trees marking every depression or watered valley. Lastly, you come out into the busy life of Kodaikanal, with street markets, fruit and vegetable shops, churches and schools, a boating lake, pretty gardens and lush meadows.

"But all the busy life is very small compared with the everlasting grandeur of the hills. From the steep escarpment you can see the southern plain laid out like a map, and at night the towns of Periyakulam and Theni twinkle like star cities. Or you can look down on an almost unbroken stretch of cloud which seems like the sea dashing against the rocks, but with sudden clefts and chasms revealing green valleys and farmlands far below."[28]

This once-quiet hill station, a refuge for missionaries from the

---

[28] *A Hill Station 1988*

plains during the hot weather, was in Dora's time becoming very popular. Its increasing popularity was helpful to Seva Nilayam, as they had a growing market for their silk-cotton quilts, jackets and teddy bears through the Goodwill Craft Shop, which sold a variety of handicrafts from projects in the plains. She was fortunate to see it before the advent of mass tourism brought increasing numbers of day-trippers and tourists and with them the inevitable traffic jams, congestion and pollution, especially during the "season", with many of the attractions described by Dora now spoilt by litter and erosion.

On a visit to a model farm close to the tip of India Dora could not resist the temptation to visit Cape Comorin (Kanyakumari). She writes, "It is the thought of it that is impressive – you stand looking south, with the whole of seething, struggling, poverty-stricken, aspiring India behind you, right up to the Himalayas, and before you a vast sweep of water, to east and west, and no land between here and Antarctica."

Train journeys in India are deservedly famous – Dora recounts a trip home from Trivandrum by train "right over the Western Ghats, the train panting up with two engines, through groves of coconut, pepper, teak, and unknown forest trees right up to the bare rocks, creeping along dizzy viaducts." She adds, "So fascinating was the journey that I sat it out for 11 hours on a hard, wooden seat."

> "Someone said to me, looking at the map: 'You always write about South India. But that is a very small part of the whole, just the southern tip. Do you travel around and see other places?'

> "Surely I do, but the other states of India are like other countries, which I may visit with great pleasure but which

I am not competent to write about in great depth.

"I have described a journey to Badrinath, the ancient place of pilgrimage far up in the Himalayas and near to the Tibetan border. From there I followed the downward rushing torrent of the Ganges through deep valleys and gorges, until at Hardwar the mighty river finally leaves the mountains and emerges onto the plains. People have known for thousands of years that the river was their source of life. *Hari-Dwar* means 'the door of god'. At evening pilgrims set afloat hundreds of little boats made of leaves and filled with flowers and a light burning in the centre. As I watch the brave little boats bobbing on the chill dark current, I think of all the human hopes and fears that have gone that way through the centuries.

"The vast Ganges plain was made by the silt brought down by the river. Thousands of pumps and water wheels, channels flowing between the standing crops, ploughs turning up the fertile soil, populous cities and great monuments, all owe their existence to the Ganges water. Midway in its course is the holy city of Benares [now Varanasi] where devout Hindus desire to be cremated at their death, and to have their ashes immersed in the water. Benares is probably the oldest continually inhabited place on earth and its traditions are lost in antiquity. Another five hundred miles lie between Benares and the Ganges delta. In the 17th Century there was a fishing village on the delta – one of many. It was named Kalighat from a black stone which was venerated as an image of the goddess Kali. The British East India Company set up a trading station there. Ultimately, after many battles, the British took over the whole of Bengal and the trading station grew into a city, still named after

Kali.

"It is a city of crowded slums, homeless people, dirt, beggary and destitution, but a city of power and magnificence. The British impress on Calcutta [Kolkata] is deep and the splendid buildings shine out far across the great open spaces of the Maidan. The white marble Victoria Memorial is not only a relic of the Queen-Empress, but a magnificent museum of Indian history, from the first days of the Company till the achievement of Indian independence. I stood there in the room full of the portraits of those who had worked and fought for freedom, Jawarhalal Nehru and his father, Mothilal Nehru, Rabindranath Tagore and Devendranath Tagore, Gandhi and Patel. I felt the impact of a great presence: India produced giants in those days.

"I remember, in Calcutta, the old Zoological Gardens, with Victorian iron work, and especially the bird house, so lofty that full sized trees could grow in it. The house was full of cooing and twittering, of birds courting, nesting and splashing in the stream that ran through it. I do not usually like zoos but this I can remember with pleasure.

"The great cantilever bridge spans the arm of the delta known as the Hooghli, between Howrah and Calcutta. Each morning and evening a solid mass of traffic moves across it, slowly, because there is one pace for all and the lorry must adjust its speed to that of the ragged rickshaw man. In the damp winter morning the mist curls on the surface of the oily and polluted Hooghli. At its source the river was turquoise blue. Here it is yellowish grey.

"At Sarnath, near Benares, and at Bodh Gaya near Patna,

I visited the scenes of the life of the Buddha. At Sarnath he preached his first sermon in the deer park and at Bodh Gaya he attained enlightenment, after his vigil under the sacred peepul tree, following an intense inward struggle to understand the meaning of life. Whether we accept his conclusions or not, there seems to be peace around us as we walk on the very pavements trodden by his feet two thousand six hundred years ago, or stand in the shade of the ever-tremulous leaves of those trees, said to be descended from the original peepul tree.

"Delhi, now restored as the capital of free India, is full of the Mogul splendour, but one thing left a deeper impression on me than even Akbar's Marble Court and his throne of justice. In old Delhi is a Sikh temple built on the spot where a great hero and defender of the Sikhs was martyred. At every hour of the day a vast crowd gazes reverently at the *Granth*, the Sikh bible, displayed with great honour. You leave your shoes outside the temple, as is customary, but they are taken in charge, not by a paid boy, but by a young Sikh of good family, taking his turn of voluntary service. It is part of the Sikh religion to show hospitality to travellers, so, in a huge kitchen adjoining the temple you may eat freshly cooked chapatis and dahl, and no questions asked, while the same young men carry the sacks of wheat flour on their backs. The sense of a strong community is overwhelming.

"At the Taj Mahal, only a few hours journey outside Delhi, you can watch the tourists who come from every country in the world. There are Americans and Japanese, Germans and Danes, mostly with odd-looking clothes and cameras and binoculars slung around them. There are conventional middle-class Indian families, the mothers in silk saris and the children in shoes and socks. Occasionally there is an Indian farmer with his family, quiet and overawed. The endless day-long stream of tourists flows up the central path of the beautiful formal garden, mounts the platform in front of the Mausoleum, and then appears to be sucked down into the vault, to emerge a few minutes later. The tourists haggle with the shoe-minders and wrestle with the straps and buckles, then back down the central path. Just one last snap, 'Us in front of the Taj' and they are gone. Meanwhile you can sit in peace by the old sandstone buildings that flank the court, under the great trees, with only the darting squirrels for company, and watch the fun, while the presence of the queenly Taj shines over all.

"Then there is Jaipur with its Rajput palaces, so rich in architectural beauty that only a fragment of it can be kept in order. I have seen magnificent carved gateways leading onto ironsmiths' yards, and I have found an old house enshrining a marble temple used only as a shelter for goats and a nesting place for flocks of doves.

"There is Udaipur with its five calm lakes among low hills, and far, far, out, beyond the desert, is the strange city of Jaisalmer with a vast fortress, and the most richly carved house frontages I have seen in India. For what does it exist, apart from the fame of ancient conquest? It lies in a vast tract of country where it rains once a year and sometimes not even that, and where very little will grow, and the only occupation seems to be camel breeding.

"I could go on writing for days and weeks always finding something new. But we are on the tourist route. If we leave that, we can see the daily work of India, as it really is. We can see hundreds of miles of cultivated land without anything larger than a village; we can see the plough and the ox cart, the bent backs of toilers, the quarry men and wood-cutters, the shabby buses and the cyclists and rickshaws waiting at a hundred level crossings. The tourist route with all its glories is only a thin line across the vastness of India. And that vastness is not one world or one society: there are thousands of castes, tribes and communities; myriads of interlocking traditions and customs, superstitions and philosophies. There are saints and prostitutes, swindlers great and small, corrupt officials and faithful servants, seekers of truth and dealers in lies. The Government itself remains on the fringe; the mainspring of life is from within. Life is an ever-growing tree with countless branches. Kings and statesmen die, but life continually renews itself."[29]

"Pilgrimages are still a feature of Indian life; you may see men dressed in little but an orange *lunghi* and a headscarf, carrying shoulder bags, and festooned with *malas* (sacred beads) all along the roads leading to the Palani Temple during the pilgrimage season. If you stop and talk to them, they may be bank clerks, Government employees or medical workers, but all are equal before Murugan, the god who rides on a peacock and is a favourite in Tamil Nadu. Many have given up drinking, sex and other indulgences in the period leading up to the pilgrimage, which may be in a crowded minibus, or by means of a long walk on hot and dusty roads.

These pilgrims, and indeed many worshippers at festivals for village deities, may stick skewers through their cheeks or

---

[29] *More of India 1982*

tongue, carry fire pots, walk on burning coals or carry decorated frames secured by metal hooks in their skin. The drums leading the procession seem to induce a kind of hypnotic state where pain is not felt. It can be a surprise to see, as the devotees dance past, someone smeared with ash, eyes half-closed, in a trance, holding a clay pot of glowing coals, and realise it is the man who served you in the teashop the other day or the woman who brings her children to the clinic.

Reflecting on her many experiences of travelling in India, Dora brings our attention back to the "minute speck" which is Seva Nilayam. Like Voltaire, faced with intractable moral and philosophical questions, Dora's response is to cultivate the garden, and to attend to the daily needs of those around her in the most practical of ways. She addresses the many readers of her *Letters from Seva Nilayam*:

"I write to you six times a year about Seva Nilayam, and I am always very happy at your response, and very grateful, too. As my daily life is here, this place has become a small world of its own to me, surrounded by its hills, ravaged by drought or storm, and beset by human sorrows and needs.

"Yet it is a minute speck on the map of India, less than a grain of dust. To reach the north of India you can travel three days and three nights by train, and after that, you will feel in your very bones the vastness of it. You cross enormous, dusty plains, where villages of low huts cling to the earth, and you go through towns where the new and garish jostles the old and decayed. There are great rivers, which are sometimes only wastes of sand, sometimes terrifyingly in spate; temples hidden in shady groves, sugar refineries and spinning mills, and cement and chemical works pouring out dust and fumes. Loaded bullock carts wait at level crossings, and there are bicycles, bicycles, and more bicycles. There are new, clean, white colleges, and classes of village children sitting under trees, near the school of mud and thatch which is too small to hold them. All these fly by, as the train goes on, for three days. What is Seva Nilayam? It has never been heard of. Its name, even, is in a different language, Tamil, the language of the South.

"In India there are many, many hospitals, doctors, clinics, and leprosy treatment centres. A few we know; the great majority we know little or nothing about. There are areas where medical treatment is very thinly spread, and there are people who have to go miles walking, or on bullock carts, to get help. There are tribes living in jungles. It is like this in the area served by Seva Nilayam, and we know it is so in many parts of the country. It can be daunting to break down the walls of one's little world by such travel. One returns to the familiar scenes with a mind still bemused by the sense of distance, and the countless pictures of the country, momentarily seen, but sharply remembered. It is salutary to feel like this, and not to believe the world began or will stop with one's own concerns. But at the same time, it is necessary to adjust the focus to the nearer scene, and the daily work. The great Indian poet, Kabir, speaks of the human soul like this:

Within this earthen vessel are powers and groves and within it is the Creator; within this vessel are the seven seas and the unnumbered stars; the touchstone and the jewel appraiser are within."[30]

---

[30] *The One and the Many 1976*

Dora with Mr Reddy, Seva Nilayam Silver Jubilee 1988

Chapter 13

THE STORY OF DORA'S LATER YEARS

In 1995 I stayed for two weeks at Seva Nilayam, delighted to find Dora still much the same as she had been in 1987 when I left my Varusanadu village to return to the UK. She was, however, by then extremely deaf, and the hearing aids she had were less than perfect, and I had the dubious pleasure of bellowing out, at her request, passages from *Cold Comfort Farm* each evening before Dora went to bed. The patients would peek out of the ward windows wondering what the noise was. My attempts to abbreviate the story were noticed and not appreciated. "You have missed a bit!" Dora would complain. She involved herself, still, in the life of Seva Nilayam but her mobility was poor and she depended on the untiring care of Gnanambal, a disabled woman who had worked at Seva Nilayam for many years. The three of us spent Easter at a local convent where the sisters provided us with rooms and a wheelchair for Dora to attend the services. One evening as I left, she said with a smile, "You know what I like about you, Caroline? You never try to kiss me goodnight!" I wondered whose presumptuous behaviour had occasioned her remark.

The story of all Dora's years in India is inextricably linked with her relationship with Seetharama Reddy, the young farmer who, with his wife, took the extraordinary step of moving with a middle-aged Englishwoman he had only known for a short time to a remote part of Tamil Nadu to start a social work project.

Mr. Reddy (as he was always addressed by expatriates) was, at the time Dora met him, under pressure from his family to take another wife: he had been married to Hamsa for some time and no children had been born. He must have seen Dora's suggestion as an opportunity to move away, to save his marriage, and perhaps to do something interesting and pioneering. As foreigners were not allowed to buy land in India, Reddy was essential for the purchase, and as Dora had no money, he put up the funds necessary. From Dora's thankful letter to Laci Gondor in February 1963 it appears her Hungarian friend also contributed some money as a loan towards the purchase. The land was relatively cheap, as the area was barren and featureless; later Reddy was paid back the cost of the purchase of Seva Nilayam's land (about 2 acres). He also had an eight-acre plot for himself. A small house was built for the Reddys on the Seva Nilayam plot, adjoining his land. In due course Hamsa gave birth to two girls, Meera and Renu, and Dora was delighted to take on the status of *patti* (grandmother).

Reddy in many ways translated and mediated India to Dora; he was a very good friend and helper to her at Mudichur, when she must have often felt out of her depth. She calls him "my best friend" in a letter to Alison, and writes, "This young man was very willing to work and ask for nothing in return but only wished to see the clinic flourishing." Now, in a rough area populated by the "robber caste" Thevars, she needed him to communicate with local people, to be her interpreter, (her Tamil was never more than basic) and to lead the work of setting up the farm and clinic. She writes approvingly of his willingness in those days to strip off to his vest and shorts and join the labourers. Through his contact with foreign volunteers and his lively intelligence, he became fluent and colloquial in English. He made regular visits during the communal meals in the kitchen (he took his meals at home): I remember he would come through the door that linked his house with the Seva Nilayam kitchen saying "Sorry for the disturb," and then sit

181

down to regale the company with the latest local gossip.

He knew, and Dora never tired of repeating, that without him Seva Nilayam would never have come about; a certain sense of entitlement was obvious and inevitable. As John Dalton notes, "You need local people around you. You need a fixer."

Reddy's behaviour was rooted in his caste origins and despite Dora's beliefs in equality and diversity he never let anyone forget his higher status. Dalton recalls witnessing an encounter between Reddy and some rich and powerful local Dalit farmers where Reddy was reclining on his string cot and the farmers were sitting on the floor, not offered chairs or refreshment. ("Or if they had been", he remarks, "they would have been given special tumblers.") When Hamsa sent food to Reddy in the field, she would never send it with the Dalit who was the usual errand boy. So despite Dora's insistence on treating all alike, these principles were not shared by her main collaborator.

As Dora became older the trustees of the Village Service Trust (VST), set up by previous volunteers in the UK to support Dora's work, were anxious to find a way to keep the work going. The Ryder Cheshire Foundation (RCF) had a focus on TB, which had always been a concern of Dora's. She had actually met Group Captain Leonard Cheshire in the past and was impressed by his work. VST trustees met representatives of RCF in 1991 to create a structure which would outlast Dora. Funding was eventually agreed for a TB ward and for a Director.

It was difficult, however, for Dora to accept that things would have to change. Patsy Wright-Warren, the RCF Projects officer, found Dora to be "a small Liverpudlian woman who clearly had a strong character and total dedication to the centre" with "a strong belief that 'small is beautiful'". She noted that Dora was unhappy at losing control, and that Reddy was "fiercely resentful".

RCF were now the major funders so they had a huge influence. They looked closely at the farm accounts and pointed out that the salary Reddy was receiving as farm manager was out of proportion to the farm income. Long-term volunteers had always suspected that Reddy expropriated a lot of the farm produce for himself. When RCF became involved, it was observed that, for the first time, all the Seva Nilayam rice came into the Seva Nilayam store-room, and was locked in. With Reddy side-lined, (Dora wanted him to be on the committee, but he could not be both farm manager and committee member, so he opted for farm manager, thus keeping the farm but losing his influence), the kitchen bills mysteriously halved. When Dora asked the new director why this should be, he enigmatically replied: "Perhaps you should be asking why they were so high before."

First one, then a second director appointed by RCF felt Reddy's influence: if they told anyone to do anything, it would be checked with Reddy first; conflicts arose. Increasingly marginalised and outmanoeuvred, Reddy's influence over Dora meant little now she had withdrawn from active involvement in the clinic. One of the many changes imposed by RCF was an outreach programme creating health guides in the villages. This had always been resisted by Dora, who wanted the clinic to serve those who came; to be, as she said, "a place you turn to when you need help". She was dismissive (or perhaps had seen no good examples) of the value of training health workers in villages to prevent health problems arising. There was also a change in governance at Seva Nilayam with a new committee and new general body members, including local businessmen.

Seva Nilayam was now "in association with Ryder-Cheshire Foundation" and appointed a new director. Dora was now increasingly frail and confined to her room. In the files are letters from the RCF director and from Patsy Wright-Warren to Dora, from 1993, expressing dismay at Dora's unhappiness with the changes.

Despite a Letter (No 2 of 1994) stating defiantly "Seva Nilayam has pursued a line of its own during all these years and does not intend to change," things were changing rapidly. She was heard to say plaintively: "We want our clinic back!" ('We' meaning her and Reddy) and on more than one occasion asked Dalton, "Please be nice to Mr. Reddy." On my visit in 1995 Reddy bitterly laid out a long list of complaints about RCF. From Dora's letters to Tony Huckle at VST it seems one of her responses to the changing circumstances and loss of control of Seva Nilayam was the decision in 1994 to register her own trust, The Dora Scarlett Trust for Baby Welcome Home, which would be able to raise its own funds independently of VST and RCF and address the issue of female infanticide.

At the end of 1994 the first News from Seva Nilayam written by Director Vijayaraman appeared. He states: "After associated (sic) with Ryder-Cheshire Foundation, Seva Nilayam showed steady progress especially in the outreach programme. In the past eight months a new working culture is created and we are able to move into a new direction which is really needed for the welfare of the poor." The eight-page booklet, with poorly reproduced photographs and many spelling mistakes, shows fundamental changes taking place. Whereas once Dora wrote "figures have no place in our work," there are three pages devoted to statistics: "Number of clinic days: 208; number of outpatients treated: 29,976" and so on; rather touchingly, the individual was not completely lost in the blizzard of figures:

"Number of patients received monitering assistant for treatment (sic): 17 (including the kidney patient Mayandi Pandi)."

The newsletter also includes a report on an event not commented on in her letters by Dora: on the 1st of June 1994 she was awarded the MBE "for her services to the poor and sick for more than three decades". The award was presented at Seva Nilayam by the British Deputy High Commissioner. Alison wrote to congratulate Dora and, in a typically astringent comment, said that whilst the OBE might stand for "Other Buggers' Efforts" she was sure that in Dora's case the MBE stood for "My Bloody Efforts!"

Seva Nilayam had been set up as a Registered Society in 1963 with a general body of members who elected an executive committee. Dora was for many years the Secretary-Treasurer. (It is not hard to imagine that her previous experience setting up Communist groups in Southern England during and after the war came in useful; John Dalton recalls at one point asking, in fun, if she was running a Registered Society or a secret society and she replied after some thought, with a smile, "Sometimes I think a secret society is better!") I myself was a member of the committee for several years. Dora chose committee members who she knew and who were sympathetic to her principles, but over time these supporters dropped away and were replaced with associates of Dr Ramesh Rao, a long- time member of the committee.

Letter No 3 of 1994 is entitled *Jeya*, and tells of a friend of Dora's who lived in Madras, a follower of the Theosophist, Annie Besant, who had also known Maria Montessori, the pioneering educational innovator. Jeya had been involved in a Baby Welcome Home which, it seems, provided maternity care and rescued unwanted infants. The practice of female infanticide was prevalent throughout the area around Seva Nilayam and Dora believed that,

"The title Baby Welcome Home would give us the means to teach that every child is precious and that even from the day of birth, the child is a full human being with human rights and capacities. ...The Government has recently started a project entitled *Cradle* and has invited the parents of unwanted babies to place them in a basket so that they can live and be cared for in the Government home but while we welcome this we think it is better that parents would feel their own responsibilities and should be aided to overcome their difficulties by family planning."

This is the last Letter I can find under Dora's name in the format and style of her previous Letters. The following year the Dora Scarlett Trust for Baby Welcome Home – a voluntary organisation giving free maternity service in rural areas, sent out its News Letter Number One for 1995 entitled "How it began?" with a stylised and typically Indian 'mother and child' vignette in the heading. The letter does not sound much like Dora and has many spelling mistakes, but this had been a feature of her Letters for some time, much bemoaned by myself and Alison. She writes:

"Our chairman [Lion Dr Ramesh Rao] has long been very keen on having a good maternity service as the nearest maternity hospital is 15 miles away by road at the same time we believe that to fight against infanticide. (sic) We must have something positive to teach and to offer, we therefore want to make Aundipatti a place where lives are saved and not destroyed and we wish to call it often [after] a home once run by a dear friend of mine in Madras, the Baby Welcome Home. There are 6 acres of good land centred on Aundipatti and we have a chance to buy these but it will be a very hard pull to raise the money."

A further document appears from the Dora Scarlett Trust for Baby Welcome Home entitled "Out of the Dark Ages" and briefly outlines once again the reasons for setting up the Home. It is a confused and rambling piece about the status of women and the practice of female infanticide. Later Dora had to apologise for it:

"Dear Friends, I have been rather behind with my letter writing lately and also I have to apologise for one News Letter which I am told was very badly written. The person who took the dictation was seriously over-worked and I cannot check it myself as my eyesight is not good now. Several people said it could not have been written by me because of all the mistakes in it."

The letter goes on once again to explain why a maternity service and baby home is necessary and gives a few more details about the land: "There is a very suitable 6-acre piece of land which we want to buy, central to Aundipatti, already having a water supply and 2 buildings. ...we want to keep the project quite flexible so that as time goes on, we shall discover the most effective way of action, whether through maternity services, a foster home or both but the essential must be an atmosphere of loving care."

Yet another newsletter turns up in May 1994. This newsletter mentions female infanticide, the marriage of close relatives (which leads to deformities), under-age marriage, the blaming

187

of women for the impotency of their husbands, ("such girls are thrown out to earn their own living for no proper examination is made about the impotency. With such marriages the girls' health is ruined. The young husbands find the girls misfit for conjugal felicities and some of them become polygomists (sic).")

It is no wonder that Alison writes in August 1994: "The appeal for your new Baby Welcome Home is so badly printed that it is only just possible to make out what it's about."

The project had little support from Village Service Trust. By the 1990s fewer people were actually practising infanticide because ultrasound scans were available, allowing female babies to be detected and aborted, so in fact the Baby Welcome Home was an out-of-date solution. In the end the project came to nothing: a letter from 1995 advised donors that they had stopped raising funds. In 2000 VST wrote to supporters to inform them that any money raised had been transferred to Seva Nilayam, and reassured them that maternal and child health and welfare continued to be a priority for the clinic.

Until Dora's death, VST along with RCF continued to fund the TB work, the outreach and the daily clinic, working with the director, and eventually integrating this into a wider health and development programme known as Network Theni, working with a number of local organisations, with a respected programme adviser, and strong management support from Arogya Agam.

This episode shows how frail and vulnerable Dora had become. Her health had deteriorated: in 1992 she had breast cancer and a mastectomy, (she wrote to me that same year "I am quite well and have been under the scan and there are no problems"); in the early 1990s she also had a herpes zoster infection that affected her sight and hearing, and her mobility was reducing.

In 1995, when I was there, Reddy supervised the building of an en-suite bathroom to make things easier for her. A wheelchair was cobbled together and guide rails installed to help her move about the campus. Throughout her decline she was faithfully cared for by Gnanambal, who nursed her to the end.

There has been speculation that Dora's gradual return to the Catholic Church during the 1980s and 1990s may have had some influence on the concept of the Baby Welcome Home; this was never made explicit. During the 1980s Dalton remembers her having regular meetings with a priest in Madurai (when asked why, she simply retorted, "Why do you think?") Priests and nuns visited her, she donated money for a church bell in Aundipatti, she went to Mass at the local church; when she returned from hospital in her last days she was given extreme unction and the funeral was conducted according to Catholic rites.

Reddy eventually received an ex-gratia payment, sanctioned by VST in June 1994, in return for an agreement to discontinue his involvement with Seva Nilayam, although he would continue to visit Dora. Dora was pleased with the plans to mark his retirement with this payment, but in a rare moment of self-pity complained to Tony Huckle that she felt she had been "cast off like an old shoe" with no appreciation "or even a dried bean."

By the late 1990s, with his influence on Dora minimal and his ability to benefit from Seva Nilayam curtailed, Reddy sold up and left the area. Neither he nor any members of his family were amongst the thousands who attended her funeral, despite a general belief in India that it is imperative to attend funerals of people one has known, to get a last look at the face before it disappears for ever.

In early 2001 Dora became increasingly weak and was admitted to the Grace Kennet Hospital in Madurai. Her constant refrain was "I want to go home". Dr Ramesh Rao agreed with Dalton that there was no use in what he called "heroic treatment" and so she was taken home, accompanied by Dalton and Gnanambal, in a van fitted out with a bed. Dalton recalls the difficult journey:

> "Stuck in a traffic jam on the ghat road at a railway crossing, with the sun streaming through the van window, I remember saying, 'are you all right Dora?' and she said, forcefully, 'NO!' with what might have once been a twinkle in her eye."

Installed in her room, with a drip and catheter, it was just a matter of time: priests were called, nuns visited, but she was unconscious most of the time. Gnanambal still vividly recalls the last day:

> "She had some snacks and tea but later when I tried to feed her, she refused, and asked for milk. I gave her just a little. I was sitting with her talking, telling her about my family, and she mentioned her brother, sister-in-law and brother's son. About 9.30 she had a little more to drink. I asked her to lie down, and I was just going on talking, telling her stories from *Mahabharata* and *Ramayana*, Krishna as a baby stealing the butter, and playing with the gopis. I just wanted to pass the time; I did not think she was going to die. I lay down with her, then about 10.45 she just coughed and then the breath stopped. I called everyone to come, told people to ask Director and John [Dalton] to come, and Dr Chandrasekar confirmed she had died. That was March 29th."

When she died, Dalton was woken up in the night by Lakshmanan with a request to go to Theni to get ice. A jeep-load of ice and sawdust was fetched and the respected Seva Nilayam doctor, Chandrasekhar, took charge of the body, (not the usual role for a doctor) and laid it out on a bed of ice. Dalton has a strong memory of that moment: "Dora looked so much younger: all the wrinkles go out of the skin in death, and she looked ten, twenty years younger, it's probably how these myths of saints looking young at the end grow up." Word of Dora's death got out and people started arriving. Dora lay in state for three days, with regular supplies of ice helping to preserve the body, which was covered in marigolds and rose petal garlands, with the face uncovered. The lying-in-state was exceptional, and normally only accorded to VIPs, but so many people wanted to see her face, and many would have to travel long distances. Dora's long-time protégé Gunasekaran and Dalton camped out at Seva Nilayam during this time, setting up an impromptu gin bar, and greeting former members of staff who had made the journey to pay their respects. The Presentation Sisters advised about the coffin and the grave: the wooden coffin had to be lined with handloom cloth, and the grave needed a brick lining to create a foundation for any future structure.

On the day of the funeral three priests and thirty nuns arrived to officiate, and the whole area took on the character of a festival, with traders setting up stalls selling candy floss, drinks and trinkets. The Mass took place, followed by fierce arguments over who would carry the coffin to the grave: in the end a very long way round was agreed, and teams of pall bearers went in relay, everyone taking turns and tripping over each other to get the coffin on to their shoulders. Dalton thought she would have loved the crowds, the jostling and the firecrackers, and the spectacle which can be seen in Gnanambal's treasured, but now faded, photos of the day. Once the coffin was lowered and its lid put on, lengthy eulogies were given in the Tamil style.

After three days the Seva Nilayam staff followed the local custom where milk is boiled and fed to the crows. So, fittingly, Dora had Hindu as well as Catholic rituals for her death. The Hindu ethos is that the death of an old person is a celebration, with dancing and fireworks: it seems very alien to the solemn Christian way; but Dora had been ready to go for some time.

A grand circular plinth with a roof of terracotta tiles was put up, and a tomb of black marble. There is an inscription in English and Tamil, with Dora's name and dates, and (at Dalton's suggestion) a quotation from Kahlil Gibran's *The Prophet*: "Work is Love Made Visible".

Dora's will made bequests to Dohnavur Fellowship (a charity dedicated to saving young girls who had been given to Hindu temples); to a centre for the rehabilitation of children with polio in Bangladesh; to the Liverpool branches of the Salvation Army and the St Vincent de Paul Society; to the Roman Catholic Church in Aundipatti; to Vasandham Society; to Seva Nilayam Society; to the charity Fourth World; to "V Kalliappan, for his children's education"; and to Gnanambal.

The new committee, led by Lion Lakshmanan, formed a plan to turn Seva Nilayam into a Nursing College, for which Government grants were available. VST disagreed with this plan, and after Dora's death they ended their support for Seva Nilayam, which has now become the Annai Dora College of Nursing, the site unrecognisable now, with a grand entrance, large buildings and little trace of Dora's flower garden. Dora's tomb stands near what is left of the Good Work Handicraft Training Centre and the nursing students put fresh flowers on it every day.

Dora's legacy lives on in Village Service Trust, which supports the work of Arogya Agam, the former leprosy hospital, which now offers care for AIDS patients and runs a number of projects working with marginalised people such as Tribals, Dalits, people living with HIV/AIDS, and rural women. Dora's protégé Gunasekaran took over the small project started by myself and my husband in 1987 in the remote Varusanadu valley, and this has become Vasandham, a centre for environmental research and rural development, running programmes for women and local farmers.

The work of the small rural project, begun in the early sixties, has evolved from handouts to human rights; as India has transformed, and standards of living and nutrition have improved, there are fewer demands for free medical care and much more need for rights-based advocacy, focusing on the empowerment of those left behind in India's rush to modernisation. The emphasis now is on addressing discrimination against Dalits, promoting women's rights, assisting with access to education for Tribal children, and doing sensitive work with teenagers living with HIV, as well as trying to ensure, through peer-to-peer work with pregnant women, that this will be the last generation of children born with HIV.

Enormous changes have taken place in rural India over the years since Dora sailed out on the SS *Oranje*. Indian village life fascinated, delighted, and exasperated her but in time she came to feel truly at home. She was one of a number of other expatriates who made India their home and led remarkable lives: among them Father Bede Griffiths, in his ashram by the sacred river Cauvery; Marjorie Sykes, the Quaker educator, who knew both Gandhi and Tagore, and had an organic farm in Madhya Pradesh; David Horsbrugh, who established and taught at a unique small rural school, Neel Bagh, in Karnataka;

and Brother James Kimpton, whose comprehensive village development programme, Reaching the Unreached of Village India, continues his pioneering work in health, education, housing and employment, and has given a home and a future to thousands of foster children. John Dalton is still living at Arogya Agam and remains closely involved in the fund-raising, research and design of their ground-breaking projects, delivered by a team of dedicated Indian staff.

By establishing a clinic offering free care for all, regardless of caste, creed or race, supported by voluntary donations, and by working to turn a barren piece of land into a productive and beautiful farm, Dora found the authentic life she had been seeking, and an opportunity to put into practice the Marxist notion of "to each according to their need" together with the Schumacher principle of "Small is Beautiful". Whilst not shying away from the harsh realities of Indian life, she celebrated the beauty of her environment and the resilience of the people, and her Letters and other writings introduced her readers to the vibrant traditional culture she lived in. She endeavoured first to understand, and then to meet, in an appropriate way, the needs of her local community, working on a human scale both in the clinic and on the farm. Some of the systemic changes she recognised as necessary to eradicate the poverty and ill-health she encountered in the clinic have now been made: there is less infant mortality; more children are in education; improved government health services have developed; there is more and better paid work in urban centres; and fewer people are dependent on day labour on the land. Vast inequalities, however, persist, along with gender and caste discrimination, corruption and poor access to justice; and the threats of climate change, rising temperatures, water stress, pollution and an increasing population multiply the challenges.

India remains the fascinating and bewildering land which challenged and delighted Dora Scarlett. Her idealism, born of profound reflection and experience, found in a remote corner of Tamil Nadu a place where the principles she had developed over a lifetime could be put into practice. As George Eliot said of one of her heroines, "the effect of her being on those around her was incalculably diffusive: for the growing good of the world is partly dependent on unhistoric acts" ... " and that things are not so ill as they might have been is half owing to the number who lived faithfully a hidden life, and rest in unvisited tombs."

Dora's Tomb

ACKNOWLEDGEMENTS

I am grateful to many people for help with this book: to my great friend John Dalton who, as a young man in the 1970s joined Dora's team as a general helper and went on to become a leprosy paramedic, and then the founder-director of Arogya Agam in Aundipatti, a pioneering leprosy hospital, now a centre for AIDS care and projects helping the most disadvantaged. Tony Huckle, founder of Village Service Trust, was an early volunteer at Seva Nilayam, and has remained faithful to the work started by Dora, raising funds for the projects which are her legacy. He provided me with much of the material used for this book, in a parcel which lay unopened for several years while I readied myself for the task. He also provided valuable comments on the text.

My thanks to Alison Selford, Dora's tireless correspondent for many years, who kindly gave her papers to Village Service Trust, and to her daughter Cathy Selford, who arranged for me to spend a fascinating afternoon with her. Thanks to Colin Hodgetts who not only read early versions and suggested a better way forward for the book, but also helped with preparing the manuscript for publication, and to June Mitchell who brought her keen editorial eye to the text.

I owe a great debt of gratitude to Rachel Marsh for saving my sanity with her expertise and for the cover design.

My Indian informants, the late Ms Gnanambal, Dora's faithful nurse and companion, Mr Vijayaraman, former Director of Seva Nilayam, Mr Lakshmanan, secretary of the Annai Dora College of Nursing, and Mr Gunasekaran, founder of Vasandham,

Varusanadu, gave me their time and their memories with great generosity. Other friends of Village Service Trust, in particular Claire Cox Chazot, sent photos and reminiscences of Dora.

Darren Treadwell at the People's History Museum in Manchester sought out invaluable documents for me in the collection. My grateful thanks to Irene Blessitt: she and her husband Neil volunteered with us in India and not only did they deliver my second daughter in our village house in 1985, but also more recently Irene read and annotated for me the voluminous correspondence between Dora and Alison.

Shaun Chamberlin, who listened patiently, one breakfast time at Schumacher College, to my ideas for the book, and encouraged me with his expertise to prepare an outline for a publisher, gave me more help than he will ever know.

Satish Kumar, who published some of Dora's letters in Resurgence magazine, has kindly provided a foreword, along with much encouragement and inspiration.

ABOUT THE AUTHOR

Caroline Walker was born in 1951. She studied French at the University of Liverpool. Two lengthy journeys around India with her first husband Keith Walker (1946 – 2003) in the early 1970s inspired a dream which was realised in 1979 when they began an eight year stay in India, working first as volunteers with Dora Scarlett and then with Brother James Kimpton in the villages of Tamil Nadu.

The family returned to England in 1987, having been offered work at the Small School in Hartland, a pioneering alternative secondary school founded by Satish Kumar. Caroline's MSc dissertation: As If Size Mattered: Education for Sustainability and the Human Scale Approach was published by South Bank University in their anthology Journeys around education for sustainability, SBU, 2008.

After 14 years at the school she left to work on community projects around Devon, moving in 2007 with her second husband Andrew Dunn to Dorset. She now lives contentedly alone, participating in community life and tending her allotment. She has made several return visits to South India which continues to enchant and exasperate her.

FURTHER READING

Dora's book about Hungary, *Window Onto Hungary*, Broadacre Books, 1957 is not widely available.

Dora's unpublished memoir will be available on the Village Service Trust website www.villageservicetrust.org.uk where Dora's Letters from Seva Nilayam will also be published.

Alison Macleod (Selford) *The Death of Uncle Joe*, Merlin 1997

Printed by Amazon Italia Logistica S.r.l.
Torrazza Piemonte (TO), Italy